TEST A

AS

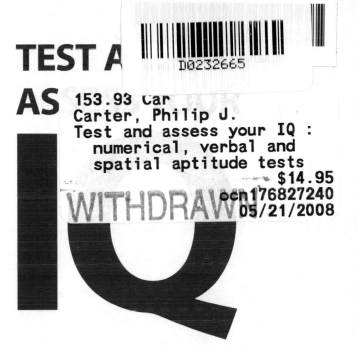

IQ

TEST AND ASSESS YOUR

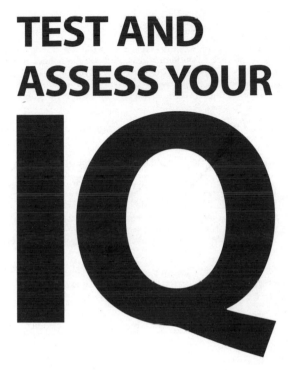

IQ

Numerical, Verbal and Spatial Aptitude Tests

Philip Carter & Ken Russell

KOGAN
PAGE

London and Philadelphia

Publisher's note
Every possible effort has been made to ensure that the information contained in this book is accurate at the time of going to press, and the publishers and authors cannot accept responsibility for any errors or omissions, however caused. No responsibility for loss or damage occasioned to any person acting, or refraining from action, as a result of the material in this publication can be accepted by the editor, the publisher or any of the authors.

First published in Great Britain in 2004 by Kogan Page Limited entitled *The Times Book of IQ Tests 4*

Reissued in Great Britain and the United States in 2008 entitled *Test and Assess Your IQ*

Kogan Page
120 Pentonville Road
London N1 9JN
United Kingdom
www.kogan-page.co.uk

Kogan Page US
525 South 4th Street, #241
Philadelphia PA 19147
USA

British Library Cataloguing in Publication Data

A CIP record for this book is available from the British Library.

ISBN 978 0 7494 5234 6

Library of Congress Cataloging-in-Publication Data

Carter, Philip J.
   Test and assess your IQ : numerical, verbal, and spatial aptitude tests / Philip Carter and Ken Russell.
      p. cm.
   ISBN 978-0-7494-5234-6
   1. Intelligence tests. 2. Self-evaluation. I. Russell, Kenneth A.
II. Title.
   BF431.3.C368 2008
   153.9'3--dc22
                                                    2007052014

Typeset by Saxon Graphics Ltd, Derby
Printed and bound in Great Britain by MPG Books Ltd, Bodmin, Cornwall

Contents

Introduction

Intelligence is the capacity to learn or understand. It is this which determines how efficiently each of us deals with situations as they arise, and how we profit intellectually from our experiences. Intelligence of course varies from person to person, and is what tests of intelligence (IQ tests) attempt to measure.

IQ is the abbreviation for 'intelligence quotient'. It is generally agreed that an individual's IQ rating continues in development to about the age of 13, after which it is shown to slow down, and beyond the age of 18 little or no improvement is found. It is further agreed that the most marked increase in a person's IQ takes place in early childhood, and theories are continually put forward about different contributory factors. For example, in recent years research in Japan has shown that the playing of computer games by children, which involve a high degree of skill and agility of mind, have resulted in higher IQ measurement.

In the last 25 to 30 years IQ tests have been brought into widespread use in industry because of the need by employers to ensure they place the right people in the right job at the outset. One of the main reasons for this is the high cost of errors in today's world of tight budgets and reduced profit margins. To recruit a new member of staff an employer has to advertise, consider each application, reduce the applicants to a shortlist, interview and then train the successful applicant. If the wrong choice has been made, then the whole process has to be repeated.

Employers also use tests to identify suitable jobs for people within an organisation. These tests can be helpful to both the employer and the candidate in identifying strengths and weaknesses, and thus help to find the job for which a person is most suited.

Such tests are designed to give an objective assessment of the candidate's abilities in a number of disciplines, for example in verbal understanding, numeracy, logic and spatial, or diagrammatic, reasoning skills. Unlike personality tests, which are also used by employers in conjunction with IQ tests, aptitude (IQ) tests are marked, and may have a cut-off point above which you pass, and below which you fail or need to be assessed again.

Although it is accepted that IQ remains constant throughout life, and therefore it is not possible to increase your actual IQ, it is possible to improve your performance on IQ tests by practising the many different types of question, and learning to recognise the recurring themes.

Besides their uses in improving performance on IQ tests, practice on the type of questions that follow in this book has the added advantage of exercising the brain. It is certainly the case that many of us do not exercise our brain sufficiently, yet it is perhaps the most important part of the human body. The intricate web of nerves of the brain somehow manages to regulate all the systems in the body, and at the same time absorbs and learns from a continual intake of thoughts, feelings and memories. It is the control centre for all our movement, sleep, hunger and thirst: in fact virtually every activity necessary for survival. Additionally all our emotions, such as aggression, love, hate, elation and fear are controlled by the brain. It also receives and interprets countless signals sent to it from other parts of the body and from the external environment. Yet it is the part of our body that many of us take most for granted.

IQ tests are standardised after being given to many thousands of people, and an average IQ (100) established. A score above or below this norm is used, according to a bell curve, to establish the subject's actual IQ rating. Because beyond the age of 18 little or no improvement in a person's IQ rating is found, the method of calculating the IQ of a child is different from the method used for an adult.

When the IQ of a child is being measured, the subject attempts an IQ test which has been standardised with an average score recorded for each age group. Thus a 10-year-old child who scored the results expected of a child of 12 would have an IQ of 120, calculated as follows:

$$\frac{\text{mental age}\,(12)}{\text{chronological age}} \times 100 = 120\,\text{IQ}$$

However, adults have to be judged on an IQ test whose average score is 100, and their results are graded above and below this norm according to known scores. A properly validated test would have to be given to some 20,000 people and the results correlated before it would reveal an accurate measurement of a person's IQ.

Like most distributions found in nature, the distribution of IQ takes the form of a fairly regular bell curve. On the Stanford–Binet scale which is widely used in the United States, half the population fall between 90 and 110 IQ, half of them above 100 and half of them below; 25 per cent score above 110; 11 per cent above 120; 3 per cent above 130 and 0.6 per cent above 140. At the other end of the scale the same kind of proportion occurs.

The tests that follow have been newly compiled for this book and are not, therefore, standardised, so an actual IQ assessment cannot be given. However, there is a guide to assessing your performance at the end of each test, and there is also a cumulative guide for your overall performance on all 10 tests.

A time limit of **90 minutes** is allowed for each test. The correct answers are given at the end of each test, and you should award yourself one point for each correct answer. Calculators may be used to assist with solving numerical questions if you wish.

Use the following table to assess your performance:

One test:

Score	Rating
36–40	Exceptional
31–35	Excellent
25–30	Very good
19–24	Good
14–18	Average

Ten tests:

Score	Rating
351–400	Exceptional
301–350	Excellent
241–300	Very good
181–240	Good
140–180	Average

Test One: Questions

1.

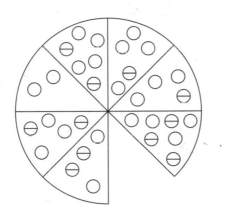

Which section is missing?

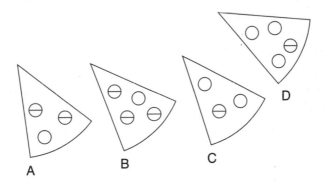

A
B
C
D

2. Which word is most opposite in meaning to *dreary*?

    practical, joyful, interested, alert, vivid

3. What number should replace the question mark?

    52, 25, 77, 77, ?, 451, 605

4. Which of the following is not an anagram of an ocean or sea?

    CAR INTACT

    HAY SALAMI

    ACID RITA

    ARABIC BEN

5. Which is the odd one out?

    leveret, foal, calf, buck, joey

6. What number should replace the question mark?

    15, 30, 45, 90, 135, 270, ?

7. The clues *seed/smile* lead to two words (5,4) that differ only by the omission of a single letter: grain/grin. Which two words (6,5) that differ only by the omission of a single letter do the clues *bowl-shaped cavity/provide food* lead to?

8.

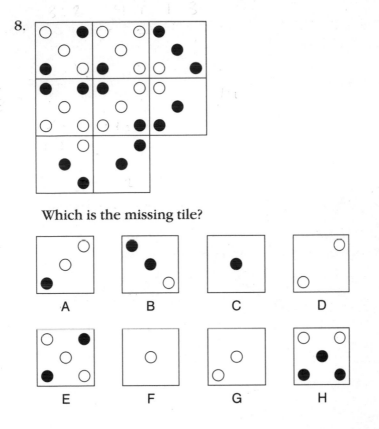

Which is the missing tile?

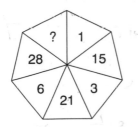

A   B   C   D

E   F   G   H

9. Semibreve is to whole as crotchet is to which of: eighth, sixteenth, quarter, half, double?

10. What number should replace the question mark?

11. The following clue leads to what pair of rhyming words (4, 7 letters)?

    every cry

12.

7	4	11	15
2	?	?	8
9	?	16	23
11	?	21	31

Which of the following is the missing section?

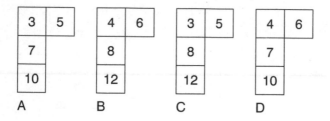

3	5
7	
10	

A

4	6
8	
12	

B

3	5
8	
12	

C

4	6
7	
10	

D

13.

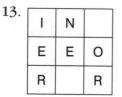

I	N	
E	E	O
R		R

Start at one of the corner squares and spiral clockwise round the perimeter, finishing at the centre square to spell out a nine-letter word. You must provide the missing letters.

14. Which is the odd one out?

15. GIANT WEB is an anagram of which two words that are similar in meaning?

16.

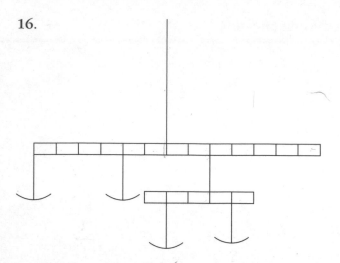

You have four weights of 1 g, 2 g, 3 g, 4 g. Place these weights into the pans, one per pan, so that the scales balance.

17. Which word, when placed in the brackets, will complete the word on the left and start the word on the right?

SC (– – –) LE

18. Insert the numbers 2 to 6 in the circles (1 is already placed) so that for any particular circle the sum of the numbers in the circles connected directly to it equals the value corresponding to the number in that circle, as given in the list. Example:

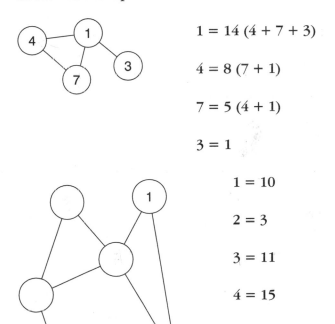

$1 = 14 \ (4 + 7 + 3)$

$4 = 8 \ (7 + 1)$

$7 = 5 \ (4 + 1)$

$3 = 1$

$1 = 10$

$2 = 3$

$3 = 11$

$4 = 15$

$5 = 7$

$6 = 5$

19. MNOP is to TSRQ as EFGH is to ?

20. Change the position of four of the words in the sentence below so that it makes complete sense.

    Great is something most of us achieve for in our lives and many of us will go to long lengths to control it.

21. Fill in the missing letters to find a profession.

    – – – CKLA – – –

22. Make a six-letter word from these four letters:

    I V Y F

23.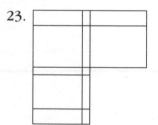

    Which is the missing box?

    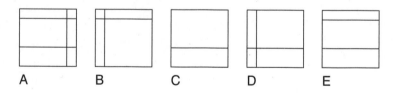

    A   B   C   D   E

24. Find an antonym for *extol* from:

    applause, denigrate, assuage, mien

25. Find a word which when placed on the end of the first word and the start of the second makes two new words or phrases:

    MASTER (– – – – –) ROOM

26. Find the two words that are closest in meaning:

    tranquil, placid, tremor, transgress, tacit, aptitude

27. What is a *merle*?

    a) blackbird
    b) boat
    c) tunnel
    d) beach

28. What number comes next?

    482, 693, 714, 826, 937, ?

29. Find two words (8, 5) in this diagram. Letters are traced across the circle by chords. If the next letter is four letters or less away it will be found by tracing around the circumference. Clue: keep it away from electricity.

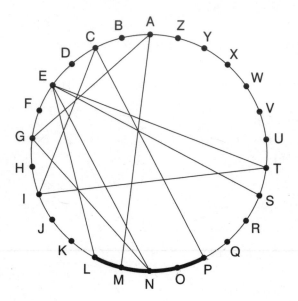

30. What number should replace the question mark?

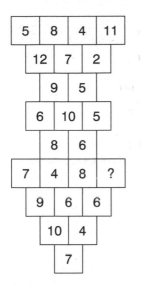

31. Fill in the missing letters to produce a mathematical term. Clue: shape.

    – – – MB – – –

32. Fill in the missing letters to produce the names of fish:

    BA – – A C – – A

    – AR – – C – U – A

33. What is *urbane*?

    a) civil
    b) outlying
    c) unruly
    d) make amends

34.

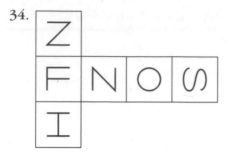

When this shape is folded to form a cube, which is the only one of the following that *can* be produced?

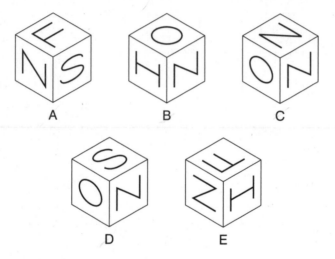

35. Fill in the missing letters to produce two words which are building terms:

PO – TC – L L – –

EM – – NK – – NT

36. Glance, namely, emboss, ? , ejects. Which of these words is missing?

    abhors, object, celery, socket, tripod

37. Simplify + 6 – 22 × 3 – 8

38. Find a word which makes two more words when added at the end of the first word and the start of the second word.

    CAN (– – –) SURE

39.

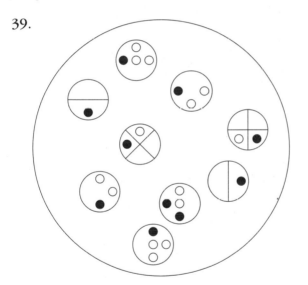

    Which circle is missing?

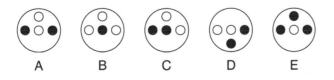

    A   B   C   D   E

40.

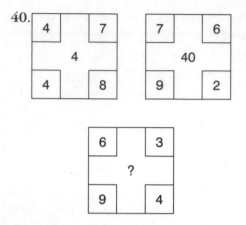

What number should replace the question mark?

Test One: Answers

1. C: added together, opposite segments contain six empty circles and three with a stripe

2. joyful

3. 154: reverse the previous number and add; for example 52 reversed is 25, and $52 + 25 = 77$

4. HAY SALAMI = HIMALAYAS. The oceans and seas are ANTARCTIC, ADRIATIC, CARIBBEAN.

5. buck: it is a male animal. The others are all names of young animals.

6. 405: multiply by 2 and 1.5 alternately

7. crater/cater

8. F: looking across and down only same-coloured dots in the same position in the first two squares are carried forward to the end square, but they change from black to white and vice versa

9. quarter

10. 10: start at 1 and working clockwise, jump one segment adding 2, 3, 4, 5, 6, 7

11. each screech

12. A: looking across and down each number is the sum of the previous two numbers

13. reinforce

14. B: A is the same as F rotated, C is the same as G and E is the same as D

15. gnaw, bite

16.

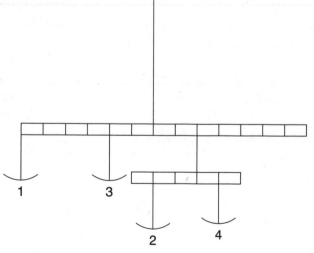

17. amp, to produce scamp and ample

18.

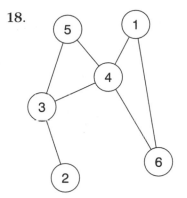

19. LKJI: LKJI follows EFGH in the alphabet, but in reverse order

20. **Control** is something most of us **long** for in our lives, and many of us will go to **great** lengths to **achieve** it.

21. BRICKLAYER

22. VIVIFY

23. E: the lines within the large square are drawn top, bottom, middle left and middle bottom

24. denigrate

25. CLASS: MASTERCLASS/CLASSROOM

26. tranquil, placid

27. a) blackbird

28. 148: the numbers 48269371 are being repeated in the same sequence

29. MAGNETIC POLES

30. 9: looking across, lines containing 1 number total 7, lines of 2 numbers total 14, lines of 3 numbers total 21 and lines of 4 numbers total 28

31. RHOMBOID

32. BARRACUDA

    BARRACOUTA

33. a) civil

34. C

35. PORTCULLIS, EMBANKMENT

36. object: each word starts with the middle two letters of the previous word in reverse

37. $+ 6 - (22 \times 3) - 8 = + 6 - 66 - 8 = -68$

38. TON: CANTON/TONSURE

39. D: each circle has an identical pairing, albeit rotated

40. 3: $(3 \times 9) - (6 \times 4)$

Test Two: Questions

1. What number should replace the question mark?

   123, 124, 126, 132, 133, 136, 142, 143, 147, ?

2. Find two of the three words: BITE – REAL – FREE that can be paired to form an anagram that is a synonym of the remaining word. For example, with LEG – MEEK – NET, the words LEG and NET form an anagram of GENTLE, which is a synonym of the remaining word, MEEK.

3. Which word is missing from the brackets that means the same as both definitions either side of the brackets?

   to burn, or be burned partially (   ) any of various trout-like fishes

4. Galena is to lead as malachite is to which of: tin, copper, zinc, titanium, iron?

5.

LEFT				
13	20	4	10	3
29	8	23	17	18
2	9	6	31	21
19	22	14	11	12
24	15	25	16	27

RIGHT				
15	32	18	17	40
44	7	63	28	56
26	16	48	23	8
42	25	3	35	46
72	19	38	10	85

Multiply the second lowest odd number in the left-hand grid by the third highest even number in the right-hand grid.

6. What familiar phrase is represented by the arrangement of letters below?

S
P
L
I
T

7.

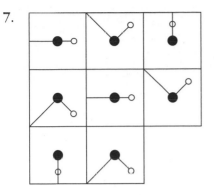

Which is the missing tile?

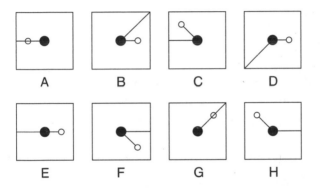

A   B   C   D

E   F   G   H

8. Which of these words is most opposite in meaning to *haughty*?

likeable, subservient, scornful, cautious, shadowy

9. Which is the odd one out?

pupil, cornea, iris, cochlea, retina

10. What number should replace the question mark?

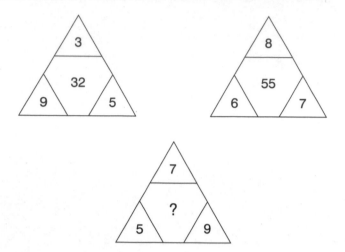

11. Put 10 of the words below together to find five items you might find in a kitchen or dining room. Two words in the list are not used.

   board, hot, screw, basin, sauce, table, plate, cup, steam, cork, pan, cloth

12. How many lines appear below?

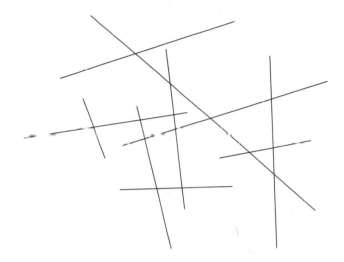

13. NOW I TOP FIVE is an anagram of what familiar phrase?
    Clue: outlook.

14.

7	10	12	13
8	11	?	14
10	13	?	16
13	?	18	19

Which is the missing section?

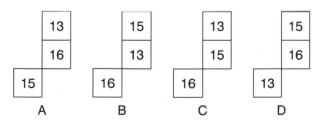

A   B   C   D

15. tap, hot, ice, sit, lad, ink, sun, ?

    Which of these words completes this list?

    arm, rib, toe, eye

16.

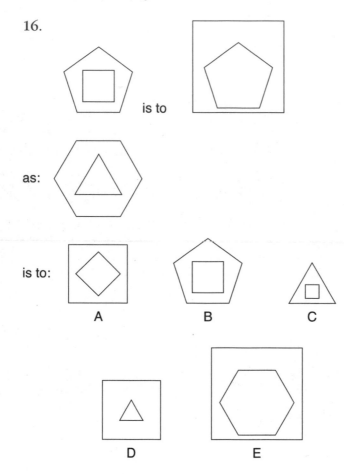

17. Which two of the following words are closest in meaning?

    consummate, profligate, conversant, licentious, disrespectful, sad

18. Use the 12 small words below to construct four longer words, each word using three of the smaller words, for example: sun + bat + her = sunbather.

    an, can, me, part, one, what, is, bar, did, so, bit, ate

19. What number should replace the question mark?

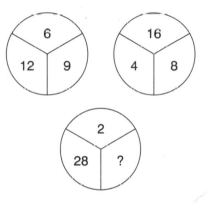

20. How many minutes is it before 12 noon if 8 minutes ago it was three times as many minutes past 9 am?

21.

74	26	69
23	12	25
39	22	46

97	24	35
26	?	17
28	19	45

Using the same logic as in the left-hand array above, what number should replace the question mark in the right-hand array?

22. Fill in the missing letters to produce the names of semi-precious stones:

    AQ – – MA – – NE

    RH – – ES – – NE

    BL – – DS – – NE

23. Fill in the missing letters to produce a name for an official:

    – – – MISS – – –

24. Find a word which when placed on the end of the first word and the beginning of the second word makes two new words or phrases.

    SHOOTING (– – – –) WARS

25. Make a six-letter word from these four letters:

    O L Y W

26. Simplify:

    $$\frac{7}{16} \div \frac{28}{32} \div \frac{4}{8}$$

27.

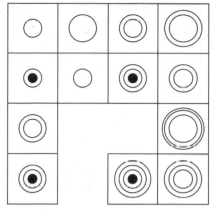

Which is the missing piece?

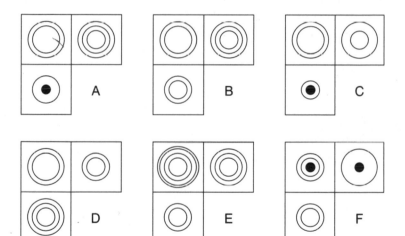

28. What is a bandanna?

    a) minstrel band
    b) Moorish boat
    c) native dance
    d) coloured handkerchief

29.

GOSPEL (MILES) IMPOSE

PSEUDO (?) TARTAN

What word is missing from the brackets?

30. Bill has £60.00 more than Alan, but then Alan has a win on the horses and trebles his money, which means that he now has £40.00 more than the original amount of money that the two men had between them. How much money did Bill and Alan have between them before Alan's win?

31. Simplify:

$-10 + 16 \div 2 + 6$

32.

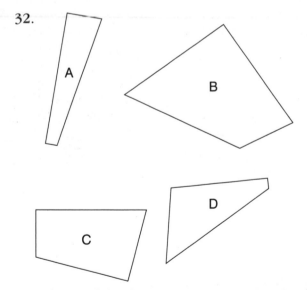

Three of the four pieces can be fitted together to form a perfect square. Which is the odd piece out?

33. Make a six-letter word from these four letters:

    O D O V

34. What comes next?

    0.49, 0.49, 0.98, 2.94, ?

35.

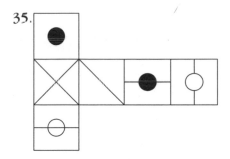

When the above shape is folded to form a cube, which is the only one of the following that can be produced?

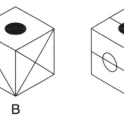

A   B   C

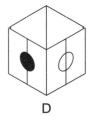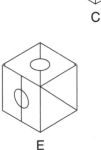

D   E

36. Rearrange the 12 letters below to spell out two fish (six letters each):

    E I L L M M N N O T U W

37. COTTAGE HAT is an anagram of what phrase (three words)? Clue: silly billy.

38. Three coins are tossed in the air at the same time. What are the chances that at least two of the coins will finish tails up?

39. What is a *nape*?

    a) loose cloak
    b) short hairstyle
    c) safety pin
    d) back of the neck

40. Find a familiar phrase in this diagram (5, 4). Letters are traced across the circle by chords. If the next letter is four letters or less away it will be found by tracing around the circumference. Clue: do not let it bite you.

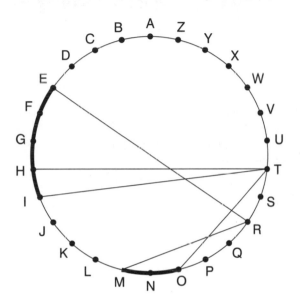

Test Two: Answers

1. 154: add the first digit to arrive at the second number i.e. 123 + 1 = 124, then the second digit i.e. 124 + 2 = 126, then the third digit etc

2. LIBERATE: FREE

3. char

4. copper

5. 432 (9 × 48)

6. split down the middle

7. E: looking across, the long line is moving 45° clockwise at each stage and the small line 45° anti-clockwise. Looking down, the reverse is happening.

8. subservient

9. cochlea: it is part of the ear, the rest being part of the eye

10. 44: (7 × 5) + 9

11. cupboard, tablecloth, hotplate, saucepan, corkscrew

12. 10

13. POINT OF VIEW

14. C: looking across, each line progresses +3, +2, +1. Looking down, each column progresses +1, +2, +3.

15. toe: take the initial letters to spell THIS LIST

16. B: the number of sides in the outer figures reduces by one, and the number of sides in the inner figure increases by one

17. profligate, licentious

18. partisan, somewhat, candidate, barbitone

19. 7: $2 \times 28 = 56$. $56 \div 8 = 7$

20. 43 minutes: 12 noon less 43 minutes = 11.17. 11.17 less 8 minutes = 11.09. 9 am + 129 minutes (43×3) = 11.09

21. 16: in each line and column the middle number is the sum of all the digits above and below and to either side

22. AQUAMARINE, RHINESTONE, BLOODSTONE

23. COMMISSARY

24. STAR: SHOOTING STAR/STAR WARS

25. WOOLLY

26. $\dfrac{7}{16} \div \dfrac{28}{32} \div \dfrac{4}{8} = \dfrac{7}{16} \times \dfrac{32}{28} \times \dfrac{8}{4} = \dfrac{2}{2} = 1$

27. B: looking across and down, an alternate circle combination is repeated with the addition of an extra circle

28. d) coloured handkerchief

29. ATONE: P S E U D O (A T O N E) T A R T A N

                5   3 1 2 3 4 5 2 1   4

        G O S P E L (M I L E S) I M P O S E

30. £260.00. Originally Bill had £160.00 and Alan had £100.00.

31. $-10 + (16 \div 2) + 6 = -10 + 8 + 6 = +4$

32.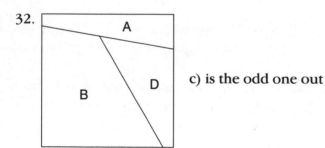

c) is the odd one out

33. VOODOO

34. 11.76: ×1, ×2, ×3, ×4

35. C

36. MULLET, MINNOW

37. ACT THE GOAT

38. It is a 50/50 chance. As it is a certainty that at least two coins will end the same side up, it is just as likely that these two coins will be tails as it is they will be heads.

39. d) back of the neck

40. TIGER MOTH

Test Three: Questions

1. Which is the odd one out?

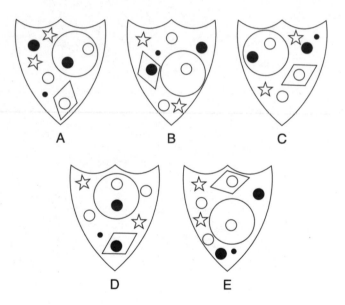

2. Which two of these words are closest in meaning?

   crave, assay, impute, examine, appoint, adhere

3. Which is the odd one out?

    annihilate, subdue, rout, crush, pulverize

4.

3	1	5	6
7	3	9	8
8	6	?	?
9	5	?	?

Which is the missing section?

10	13
12	11

A

10	11
11	10

B

9	10
11	12

C

11	10
10	11

D

5. The clues *seed/smile* lead to two words (5,4) that differ only by the omission of a single letter: grain/grin. Which two words (5,4) that differ only by the omission of a single letter do the clues *beat with/disappoint* lead to?

6. A man is playing roulette and starts with a modest value of chips. In the first 10 minutes he gets lucky and doubles the value of chips he starts with, but in the second 10 minutes he loses £20.00 in chips. In the third 10 minutes he again doubles the value of chips he has left but then quickly loses another £20.00. He then gets lucky again and doubles the value of chips he has left, after which he hits another losing streak and loses another £20.00. He then has no chips left. What was the value of chips he started out with?

7. If 9L of a C is nine lives of a cat, can you decode the following phrase?

   1 GTDA

8.

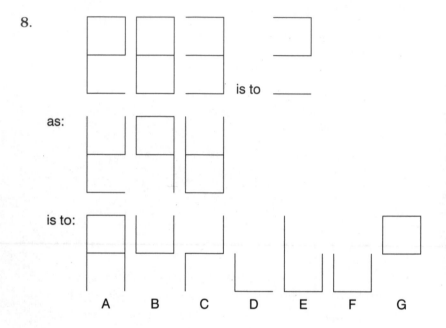

9. Presto is to fast as forte is to: loud, smooth, majestically, rigorously, slow

10. What number should replace the question mark?

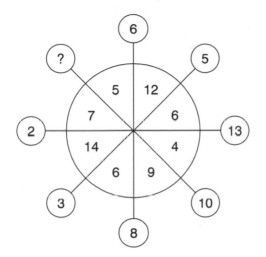

11. Which of the following is not an anagram of a word beginning with the letter A?

MEAN BILBAO

LAP DANCES

NAME A CLUB

FAIL TRICIA

12. What number should replace the question mark?

5	7	2	6			
2	1	3	2			
7	4	1	1			
3	8	6	9	7	8	3
			2	1	4	7
			2	3	1	?
			6	2	8	5

13.

What comes next?

| A | B | C | D | E |

14. Which two of the following words are most opposite in meaning?

aversion, vitality, potency, inertia, propriety, mercy

15. What number should replace the question mark?

    100, 99.5, 98, 95.5, 92, 87.5, ?

16. The following clue leads to what pair of rhyming words?

    like the wind from one side to the other

17.

38	18	1	27	21	2
9	16	26	7	6	58
28	20	3	10	32	50
15	24	11	5	36	30
19	8	17	52	13	4
12	22	42	14	44	64

What number is two places away from itself plus 2, three places away from itself multiplied by 2, four places away from itself divided by 2, and three places away from itself less 2?

18. Which word, when placed in the brackets, will complete the word on the left and start the word on the right?

    SL (– – –) HER

19. Insert the numbers 1 to 6 in the circles, so that for any particular circle the sum of the numbers in the circles connected directly to it, equals the value corresponding to the number in that circle, as given in the list. Example:

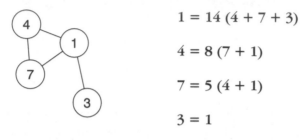

$1 = 14 \ (4 + 7 + 3)$

$4 = 8 \ (7 + 1)$

$7 = 5 \ (4 + 1)$

$3 = 1$

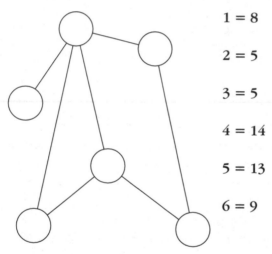

$1 = 8$

$2 = 5$

$3 = 5$

$4 = 14$

$5 = 13$

$6 = 9$

20. Change the position of four of the words in the sentence below so that it then makes complete sense.

In order to view others sympathetically we need to have aspirations with them, their character, perceive and points of empathy.

21. What is *pelota*?

    a) a ball game
    b) a fancy bow
    c) a dish of prawns
    d) a mild breeze

22. Which anagram is not a type of insect?

    TEBLEE

    AGLEBE

    FLYDOG

    DIPRES

    WRIEAG

23. Rearrange the 12 letters below to spell out two breeds of dog (six letters each):

    ABBEIO   ORSSTZ

24.

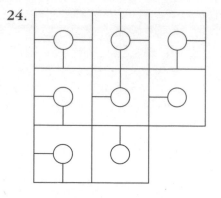

Which is the missing box?

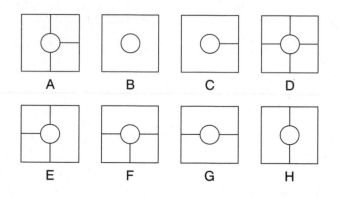

25. What number should replace the question mark?

8	2	4	2	106
7	5	3	9	132
7	8	1	2	153
3	9	5	6	131
8	1	2	7	99
9	3	1	7	?

26. Place the three-letter bits into the correct order to reveal a quotation by Tacitus (55–117 AD).

    tur tea lib als giv yis yna ent nim enb ert omu eev

27. Which number is the odd one out?

    2772

    3663

    2970

    4275

    5841

    3564

28. What is *rugose*?

    a) wrinkled

    b) reddish

    c) disguise

    d) disagreeable

29. Which two of these words are most similar in meaning?

    fallacious, abject, pestilential, baneful, mendacious, noteworthy

30. Find a word (10) in this diagram. Letters are traced across the circle by chords. If the next letter is four letters or less away it will be found by tracing around the circumference. Clue: watch out for splinters in your feet.

31. Which two pieces below can be fitted together to form a perfect square?

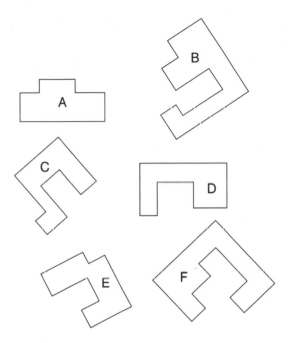

32. Which is the longest word in the English language that can be produced from the 10 letters below? No letter can be used more than once.

H U T L K E M F A N

33. What number should replace the question mark?

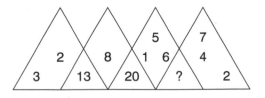

34.

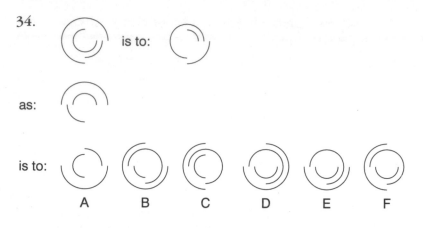

35. What is the opposite of *intractable*?

    a)   tameable
    b)   misdeed
    c)   baleful
    d)   vindictive

36. Simplify:

$$\frac{27}{91} \div \frac{54}{13} \div \frac{9}{13}$$

37. Fill in the missing letters to produce the name of a colour:

    $-\,-\,-$ AMAR $-\,-\,-$

38. Which is the opposite of plethora?

    a)   scarcity
    b)   satisfy
    c)   surfeit
    d)   copious

39. Which number is the odd one out?

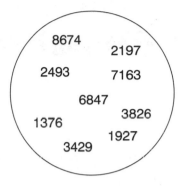

40. Fill in the missing letters to produce the name of a sporting activity:

    – – – OBAT – – –

Test Three: Answers

1. E: it contains four white dots, the rest only contain three

2. assay, examine

3. subdue

4. B: looking across, alternate numbers are +2 and +5. Looking down they are +5, +2.

5. flail/fail

6. £17.50: £17.50 × 2 = £35, less £20 = £15, × 2 = £30 less £20 = £10, × 2 = £20 less £20 = £0

7. one good turn deserves another

8. B: only lines that appear three times in the same place in the first three figures are carried forward to the final figure

9. loud

10. 11: each adjacent group of three numbers total 23 i.e. 11 + 5 + 7; 6 + 12 + 5

11. LAP DANCES = LANDSCAPE. The A words are ABOM-INABLE, AMBULANCE, ARTIFICIAL.

12. 3: the four-figure numbers in each line of the top square are repeated in the bottom square in reverse, except that a different position digit is increased by 1 each time i.e. 5726 becomes 6285, 2132 becomes 2313, 7411 becomes 2147 and 3869 becomes 9783

13. B: the largest segment moves 90° clockwise at each stage, the second largest moves 90° anti-clockwise and the smallest moves 180°

14. vitality, inertia

15. 82: deduct 0.5, 1.5, 2.5, 3.5, 4.5, 5.5

16. blew through

17. 8

18. ANT: SLANT/ANTHER

19.

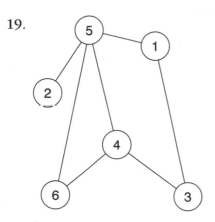

20. In order to **perceive** others sympathetically we need to have **empathy** with them, their character, **aspirations** and points of **view**.

21. a) a ball game

22. AGLEBE = BEAGLE (the others are BEETLE, DOGFLY, SPIDER and EARWIG)

23. BORZOI, BASSET

24. B: looking across and down, only lines (and the circle) that appear in the same position twice in the first two squares are carried forward to the final square

25. 128: in each line add the numbers formed by pairs of alternate digits, i.e. 91 + 37 = 128

26. Liberty is given by nature even to mute animals

27. 4275: the number formed by the first two digits plus the number formed by the second two digits is 99

28. a) wrinkled

29. fallacious, mendacious

30. SANDALWOOD

31.

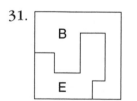

32. THANKFUL

33. 25: the numbers in the sections at the bottom are the sum of all the numbers in the adjoining triangles at the top

34. E: the arcs appear in the second figure that would complete the circles in the first figure

35. a) tameable

36. $\dfrac{27}{91} \div \dfrac{54}{13} \div \dfrac{9}{13} = \dfrac{27}{91} \times \dfrac{13}{54} \times \dfrac{13}{9} = \dfrac{13}{126}$

37. AQUAMARINE

38. a) scarcity

39. 3826: the rest are in anagram pairs, i.e. 8674/6847, 2493/3429, 1376/7163, 2197/1927

40. ACROBATICS

Test Four: Questions

1. Which two of the following words are most opposite in meaning?

   worried, tense, tepid, finite, prone, pliant

2. Cashmere is to wool as taffeta is to which of: jute, hemp, silk, cotton, linen?

3. Change one letter only in each word below to produce a well-known phrase:

   rack any fill

4. The ages of five family members total 169 between them:

   Mary and Stuart total 98 between them.

   Stuart and Margaret total 90 between them.

   Margaret and Jack total 50 between them.

   Jack and George total 33 between them.

   How old is each family member?

5. Add one letter (not necessarily the same letter) into the words below to create two new words that are similar in meaning.

   deer   dear

6. Four explorers deep in the jungle have to cross a rope bridge in the middle of a moonless night. Unfortunately the bridge is only strong enough to support two people at a time. Also, because deep in the jungle on a moonless night it is pitch black, the explorers need a torch to guide them, otherwise there is every possibility they would stumble and plunge to their deaths in the ravine below. However, between them they have only one torch.

   Young James can cross the ravine in 2 minutes, his sister Jane can cross in 3 minutes, their mother Henrietta can cross in 5 minutes; however, old Colonel Hopalong-Slowly can only hobble across in 10 minutes. How quickly is it possible for all four to reach the other side?

7.

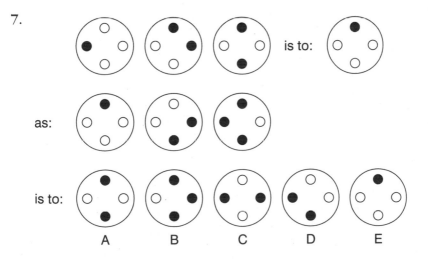

8. What number should replace the question mark?

    1, 1, 8, 4, 15, 7, 22, 10, ?

9. Which of these words is closest in meaning to *harmonize*?

    control, mar, cohere, expedite, garner

10. Which is the odd one out?

    sashay, scamper, amble, sidle, stride

11. Which two words that sound alike, but are spelt differently mean *bend/branch*?

12. The average of three numbers is 17. The average of two of these three numbers is 17.5. What is the value of the third number?

13.

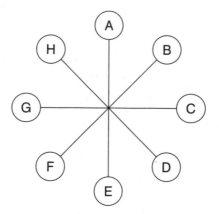

    What letter is two letters anticlockwise away from the letter immediately opposite the letter three letters clockwise from the letter F?

14.

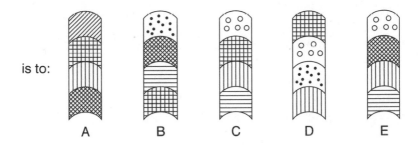

is to:

as:

is to:

| A | B | C | D | E |

15. What number should replace the question mark?

15	27
35	23

32	19
18	31

12	47
?	26

16. Only one group of six letters below can be rearranged to spell out a six-letter word in the English language. What is the word?

    KEBLOP

    EBLOGT

    DUNIRM

    TIALNC

    ARNILO

17. What is an *eagre*?

    a) a large wave

    b) an old runic letter

    c) the mouthpiece of a wind instrument

    d) an opening in a wall

    e) a fringed shoulder strap

18. Ringer, reader and lighter is a clue to which phrase (4, 4, 3, 6)?

19. What number should replace the question mark?

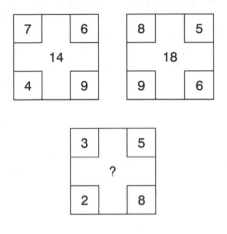

20.

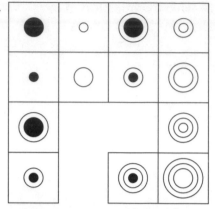

Which section is missing?

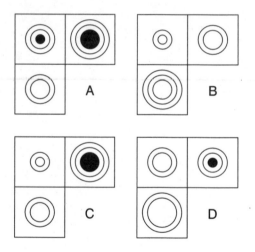

21. Find a familiar phrase in this diagram (5, 7). Letters arc traced across the circle by chords. If the next letter is four letters or less away it will be found by tracing around the circumference. Clue: fond of reptiles.

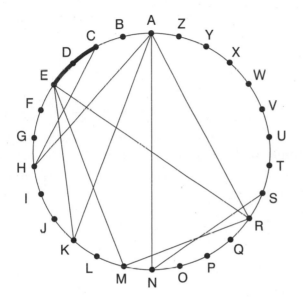

22. Which anagram is not the name of a fish?

RABLEB

NOWNIM

DOOLEP

PIKREP

BOTRUB

NUGNEL

23. What is a *binnacle*?

    a) housing for a compass

    b) commercial ship

    c) flag

    d) ski run

24. Sue, Harry and Pat have £168.00 between them. The combined amount of money that Sue and Harry have is twice as much as Pat. The combined amount of money that Harry and Pat have is the same as Sue has. How much money has each?

25. What is *retroflex*?

    a) a petrol-driven engine

    b) a returned letter

    c) a type of plant

    d) turned backwards

26. Rearrange the 12 letters below to spell out two trees (six letters each):

    ACDEHL   MNORRY

27. Make a seven-letter word out of these five letters:

    P O D E R

28. Fill in the missing letters to produce the name of a piece of furniture (4, 6):

    _ _ _ E   SC _ E _ _

29. Simplify:

$$\frac{9}{13} + \frac{18}{26} \div \frac{90}{52}$$

30. Make one eight-letter word out of two of these blocks of four letters:

    UOSO ULTI MITE WHIS

    SOCH LETE VIRT WIND

31.
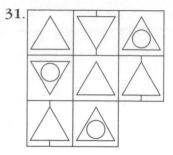

Which is the missing box?

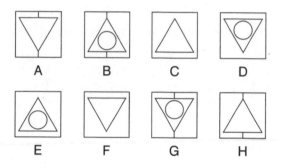

32. What number should replace the question mark?

56	3	49	27	18
74	62	19	8	35
65	92	?	34	81

33. Find a word that makes two new words or phrases when placed at the end of the first word and the beginning of the second word:

SURE (– – – –) WOOD

34. What is a *sinker*?

    a) a fishing weight

    b) a drainpipe

    c) a tool for blocked drains

    d) a type of golf club

35. How many minutes is it before 12 noon if 44 minutes ago it was three times as many minutes past 10 am?

36.

When this shape is folded to form a cube, which is the only one of the following that *can* be produced?

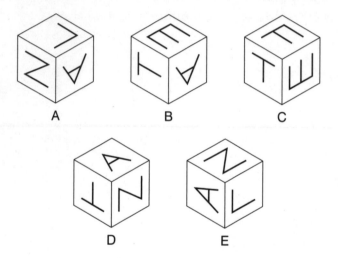

A   B   C

D   E

37. Which anagram is not the name of an animal?

    KOCOUC

    TOMRAM

    SUMSOP

    REVVET

    SELWEA

    TIKTEN

38. Rearrange the 12 letters below to spell out two nautical terms (six letters each):

    AEEEIL   MNNTZZ

39. Make a six-letter word out of these four letters:

    P I E Y

40. Make one eight-letter word out of two of these blocks of four letters:

    VIOL   WIND   TREA   IENS

    MILL   ANCE   TURE   QUOT

Test Four: Answers

1. tense, pliant

2. silk

3. rank and file

4. Mary 46, Stuart 52, Margaret 38, Jack 12, George 21

5. deter, debar

6. 21 minutes: the secret is to make sure that the fastest people do the most crossings and the slowest people the fewest. As the two slowest people are Colonel Hopalong-Slowly and Henrietta, these two should cross together. By adopting this strategy the total crossing can be achieved in 21 minutes as follows:

First: James and Jane cross	3 minutes
then: James returns	2 minutes
then: Henrietta and Colonel Hopalong-Slowly cross	10 minutes
then: Jane returns	3 minutes
finally James and Jane cross	3 minutes

7. A: only when the same coloured dot appears in the same position twice in the first three circles is it transferred to the final circle

8. 29: there are two interwoven sequences; the first progresses +7 and the other progresses +3

9. cohere

10. scamper: it is a run, whereas the others are walks

11. bow/bough

12. 16: the total of the three numbers is $17 \times 3 = 51$. The total of two numbers is $17.5 \times 2 = 35$. The third number must therefore be $51 - 35 = 16$.

13. C

14. C: top left, next to top right, next to bottom left and bottom left sections are transferred to the final figure

15. 15: the numbers in each large square total 100

16. EBLOGT = GOBLET

17. a) a large wave

18. bell, book and candle

19. 8: $(3 + 2 + 8) - 5$

20. C: looking across and down, a circle is added to each alternate square

21. SNAKE CHARMER

22. DOOLEP (POODLE). The others are BARBEL, MINNOW, KIPPER, BURBOT, GUNNEL

23. a) housing for a compass

24. Sue £84.00, Pat £56.00, Harry £28.00

25. d) turned backwards

26. ALMOND, CHERRY

27. PROPPED

28. FIRE SCREEN

29. $\dfrac{9}{13} \div \dfrac{18}{26} \div \dfrac{90}{52} = \dfrac{9}{13} \times \dfrac{26}{18} \times \dfrac{52}{90} = \dfrac{26}{45}$

30. VIRTUOSO

31. F: each line across and down contains one triangle upside down, one circle and one set of vertical lines

32. 7: the numbers in each line contain the digits 1–9 once each only

33. FIRE: SURE FIRE/FIREWOOD

34. a) fishing weight

35. 19 minutes

    12 noon less 19 minutes = 11.41. 11.41 less 44 minutes = 10.57. 10 am plus 57 minutes (19 × 3) = 10.57

36. D

37. KOCOUC (CUCKOO). The others are MARMOT, POSSUM, VERVET, WEASEL, KITTEN.

38. LATEEN, MIZZEN

39. YIPPEE

40. WINDMILL

Test Five: Questions

1. Which is the odd one out?

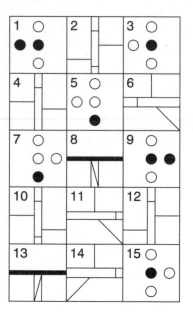

2. Which two words below are most opposite in meaning?

   wealth, equity, bias, empathy, profit, unease

3. Which two words that sound alike, but are spelt differently, mean *rapscallion/part of a church*?

4. What number should replace the question mark?

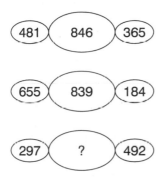

5. Change one letter only from each word to produce a well-known phrase:

    us do rate

6. Red, Amber, White, Navy, Brown, Orange, Indigo

    Change the position of two of the above colours to reveal an appropriate sequence.

7. What number should replace the question mark?

6	8	10	5
9	2	8	4
11	3	7	8
5	8	?	2

8.

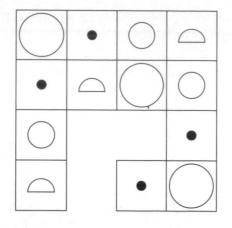

Which is the missing section?

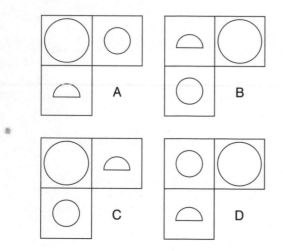

9. Which of these words is closest in meaning to *sustenance*?

comfort, solicitation, enlargement, aliment, plethora

10. Which is the odd one out?

chose, forgave, began, sung, frozen

11. Change one letter only in each word below to produce a well-known phrase:

    so court but

12. Find five consecutive numbers below that total 23:

    947251739244572561854

13.

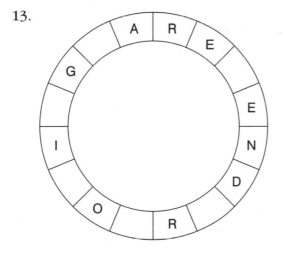

    Find the starting point and work clockwise to spell out a familiar phrase (6, 6, 4). You have to provide the missing letters.

14. What number should replace the question mark?

    1, 2, 6, 12, 36, 72, ?

15. Only one group of six letters below can be rearranged to spell out a six-letter word in the English language. What is the word?

    MECIPA

    NGEACL

    TRILOC

    FPILEN

16.  is to:

    as:

    is to:

    A   B   C

       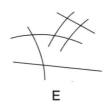

    D   E

17. Pentacle is to star as pentad is to which of: elements, period, cards, verse, dice?

18. What is a *shaddock*?

    a) a pottery fragment

    b) a water-raising apparatus

    c) a rope supporting a mast on a ship

    d) a grapefruit-like citrus fruit

    e) a small farmhouse

19. A photograph measuring 8.5 by 7.5 cm is to be enlarged. If the enlargement of the longer side is 13.6 cm, what is the length of the smaller side?

20. Complete the bottom line of letters.

A	C	E	G
D	F	H	J
G	I	K	M
?	?	?	?

21. What is an *orlop*?

    a) lowest deck of a ship

    b) firing range

    c) parapet

    d) procession

22.

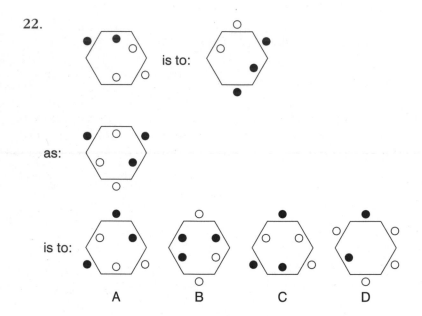

23. Which is the odd one out of:

    coyote, gopher, gerbil, ashlar

24. Which two of these words are most similar in meaning?

    idolize, odium, degenerate, opprobrium, deify, exaltation

25. Which two of these words are most similar in meaning?

    irradiate, deportment, enlighten, mendacious, calliguate, mellow

26. Find an extinct animal by moving from circle to circle, using each circle only once:

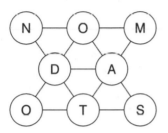

27. What is a *dobbin*?

    a) shoe polish

    b) a scratch

    c) a weapon

    d) a farm horse

28.

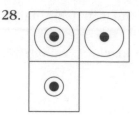

Which is the missing box?

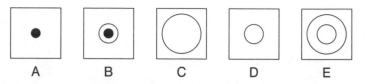

29. Which two of these words are most similar in meaning?

hermetic, hirsute, hairy, schismatic, emblematic, heretical

30. Fill in the missing letters to produce the names of two trees:

SU – – R   M – – LE

SA – – AL – – OD

31. Change one letter only in each word below to produce a familiar phrase:

seal live hit bakes

32.

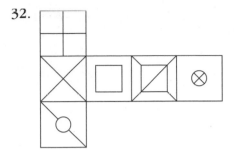

When this shape is folded to form a cube, which is the only one of the following that *can* be produced?

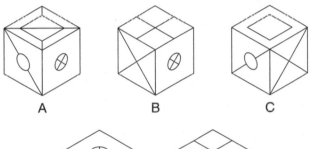

33. What number should replace the question mark?

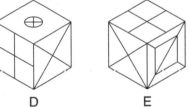

7	4	6
2	8	9
3	1	7

8	4	7
2	9	9
4	1	8

8	3	7
1	9	8
4	?	8

34. SCORE ON DEBUT is an anagram of what two words that are opposite in meaning?

35.

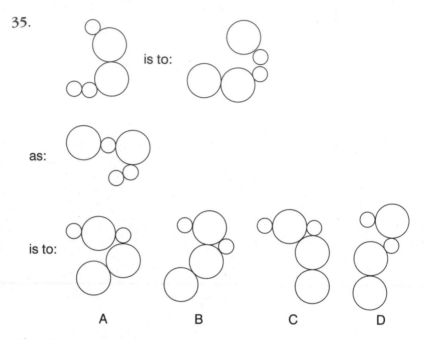

is to:

as:

is to:

A   B   C   D

36. What number should replace the question mark?

7	8	2	6
3	8	2	5
1	7	6	2
8	4	5	4

8	7	1	5
4	7	1	6
2	8	5	1
7	3	6	?

37.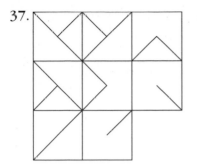

Which is the missing box?

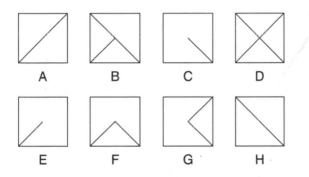

38. What number should replace the question mark?

5	6	4	8	6
2	4	2	7	9
3	7	9	5	3
1	2	9	6	8
8	4	3	5	?

39. Irate is to indignant as livid is to which of: volatile, sorry, incensed, splenetic, petulant?

40.

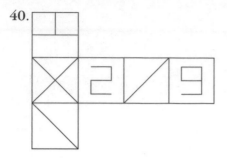

When this shape is folded to form a cube, which is the only one of the following that *can* be produced?

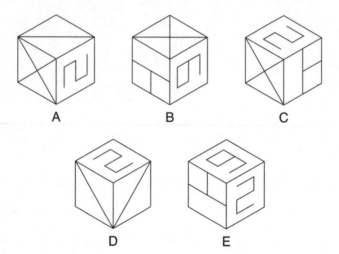

Test Five: Answers

1. 11: all the rest have a mirror-image pairing

2. equity, bias

3. knave/nave

4. 789: 29 + 49 = 78 and 7 + 2 = 9

5. up to date

6. Red, Amber, **Indigo**, Navy, Brown, Orange, **White**: so that the initial letters spell RAINBOW

7. 12: looking across and down, in each line of four numbers the sum of the first two numbers is one less than the sum of the second two numbers

8. C: so that each row and column contains one each of the four different symbols

9. aliment

10. frozen: it is a past participle, the rest are past tense

11. to count out

12. 45725

13. tender loving care

14. 216: ×2, ×3 repeated

15. NGEACL = GLANCE

16. C: straight lines turn to curved and vice versa

17. elements

18. d) a grapefruit-like citrus fruit

19. 12 cm: $(13.6 \div 8.5) \times 7.5$

20. J L N P: looking across the letters jump two places in the alphabet. Looking down they jump three places.

21. a) lowest deck of a ship

22. C: All dots that are outside in the first figure go inside on the second figure and vice versa. All white dots in the first figure turn to black in the second figure and vice versa.

23. ashlar: it is a building material, while the rest are animals

24. idolize, deify

25. irradiate, enlighten

26. MASTODON

27. d) a farm horse

28. A: looking down, the large circle disappears and looking across the smaller middle circle disappears

29. hirsute, hairy

30. SUGAR MAPLE, SANDALWOOD

31. sell like hot cakes

32. A

33. 0: from the first array to the second array the four corner and the middle numbers increase by 1. From the second array to the third array the remaining numbers decrease by 1.

34. NOTED, OBSCURE

35. A: all large circles change to small and vice versa

36. 3: looking from the first array to the second array, all odd numbers increase by 1 and even numbers decrease by 1

37. E: looking across and down, any lines that appear in the same position twice in the first two squares are cancelled out in the final square

38. 9: so that the total in each column is 19, 23, 27, 31, 35 (+ 4)

39. incensed

40. B

Test Six: Questions

1. What number should replace the question mark?

   100, 83, 66, 49, 32, ?

2.
A	C	A		
N	R	A		
H	L	T	D	E
		N	R	P
		R	E	E

   Arrange the letters in each square to spell out a nine-letter word. The two words are synonyms.

3. MILD BOARS is an anagram of which two words that are opposite in meaning?

4. Insert two letters into each pair of brackets so that they finish the word on the left and start the word on the right. The letters in the brackets, reading in pairs downwards, will spell out an eight-letter word.

    FI (- -) SS

    LI (- -) IL

    AU (- -) NK

    PA (- -) AR

5. Change one letter only in each word below to produce a familiar phrase:

    nut to ace

6. What numbers should replace the question marks?

3	6	9	2	8	3
6	3	8	2	9	6
9	2	8	?	6	9
2	9	6	?	8	2
8	3	6	9	2	8
3	8	2	9	6	3

7.

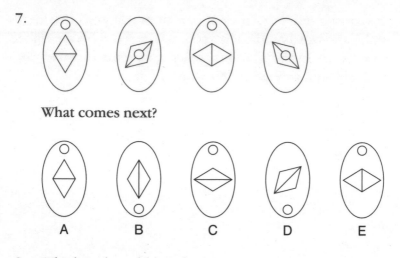

What comes next?

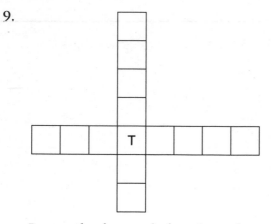

| A | B | C | D | E |

8. Which is the odd word out?

mollify, temper, indurate, mitigate, mute

9.

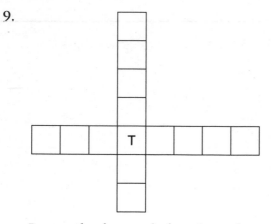

Insert the letters below into the grid to produce two related words.

A A E I I O

N P P R R R T

10. In a game of 12 players lasting for 65 minutes, three reserves alternate equally with each player. This means that all players, including the reserves, are on the pitch for the same length of time. For how long?

11. What do these words have in common?

    gardening, marionette, renown, undergrowth, existence

12. Sally has £72.00 to spend. She spends 4/9 of the £72.00 in the morning on clothes, 0.375 of the £72.00 in the afternoon on groceries at the supermarket and spends £12.00 in the evening at a restaurant. What is her financial situation at the end of the day?

13.

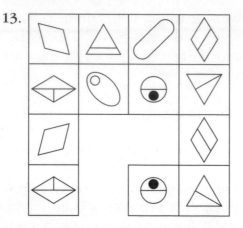

Which section is missing?

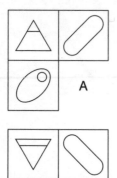

A

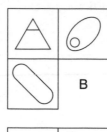

B

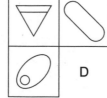

C

D

14. What number should replace the question mark?

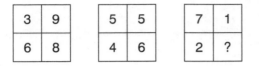

15. replenish is to refill as stockpile is to which of: provisions, furnish, cache, accumulate, supply?

16. Use each letter of the phrase REACH DARK COAL once only to spell out the names of three trees.

17. What number should replace the question mark?

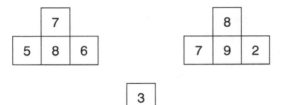

18. What well-known proverb of six words is opposite in meaning to the proverb *Many hands make light work*?

19.

A	B	C	D	E	
F	G	H	I	J	
K	L	M	N	O	
P	Q	R	S	T	
U	V	W	X	Y	Z

What letter is two letters above the letter which is four letters to the right of the letter which is midway between the letter immediately to the left of the letter V and the letter immediately to the left of the letter L?

20.

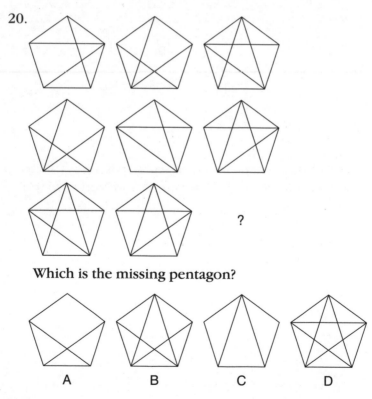

Which is the missing pentagon?

A   B   C   D

21. What is a *savoy*?

    a) a cabbage

    b) a rough bread

    c) paste for wallpaper

    d) an animal

22. Simplify:

    $-3 \times 12 \div 4 + 6$

23. Which of these words is nearest in meaning to *mystic*?

    refactory, cabalistic, tenure, obtrude

24. Fill in the missing letters to produce the name of a tree:

    – – – CKTH – – –

25. Which word, when placed in the brackets, will produce two new words with the word on the left and the word on the right?

    SUMMER (– – – – –) HOLD

26.

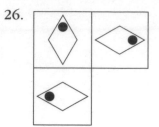

Which box is missing?

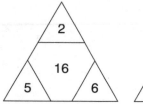

A   B   C   D   E

27. What number should replace the question mark?

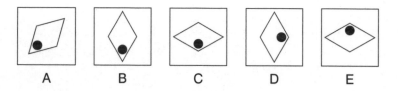

28. What is *progeny*?

a) offspring

b) a church dignitary

c) a fish

d) wild oats

29. Rearrange the 12 letters below to spell out the names of a herb and a vegetable (six letters each):

    ACEEFLN

    NORRT

30. What is a *monger*?

    a) a fish

    b) a sailor

    c) a dog

    d) a dealer

31. Which of these words is the most opposite in meaning to *affable*?

    wrangling, scruples, weird, pugnacious

32. Find two words (8, 4) in this diagram. Letters are traced across the circle by chords. If the next letter is four letters or less away it will be found by tracing around the circumference. Clue: trousers for the youngest sailor.

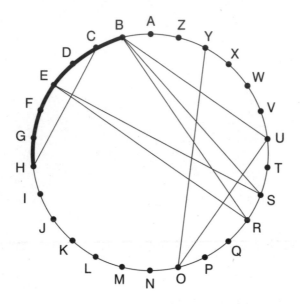

33. Which two of these words mean the same?

    depraved, disclaim, mien, degrade, implicate, disavow

34. Make a seven-letter word out of these five letters:

    F T R E I

35. Fill in the missing letters to produce the name of a drink:

    – – – UJOL – – –

36. SO DRY NICE COW is an anagram of which two words that are opposite in meaning?

37. Which word, when placed in the brackets, will produce two new words or phrases with the word on the left and the word on the right?

    BICYCLE (– – – – –) GANG

38. What is a *planchet*?

    a) a flower

    b) medicine

    c) a raft

    d) a metal disk

39.

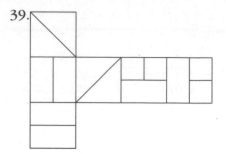

When this shape is folded to form a cube, which is the only one of the following that *can* be produced?

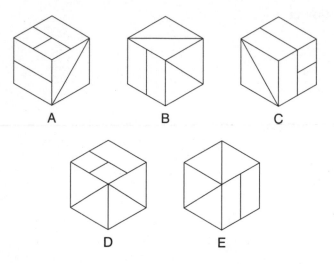

A   B   C

D   E

40. What number should replace the question mark?

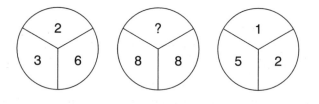

Test Six: Answers

1. 15: deduct 17 each time

2. charlatan, pretender

3. slim, broad

4. LEVERAGE: FILE/LESS, LIVE/VEIL, AURA/RANK, PAGE/GEAR

5. cut no ice

6. 3

    3

    Start at the bottom left-hand square and work along the bottom row, then back along the next row up and so on, repeating the numbers 38296

7. A: the diamond moves 45° clockwise at each stage, and the dot moves between the top of the ellipse and the middle of the diamond

8. indurate: it means to harden, all the other words meaning to soften or lessen

9. PORTRAIT PAINTER

10. 52 minutes: $\dfrac{65 \times 12}{15}$

11. They all contain numbers spelt in reverse: gard**ening**, mario**net**te, **reno**wn, undergr**ow**th, ex**is**tence

12. She has £1.00 left:

    4/9 of 72   = 32

    0.375 of 72   = 27

    restaurant   = 12

    total spend   = 71

13. D: the bottom two rows are a mirror image of the top two rows

14. 4: there are four sequences looking across the four squares: 3, 5, 7 in the top left corner, 9, 5, 1 in the top right, 6, 4, 2 in the bottom left and 8, 6, 4 in the bottom right

15. accumulate

16. CEDAR, LARCH, OAK

17. 2: $3 \times 7 = 21$

18. Too many cooks spoil the broth

19. J

20. A: looking both across and down, lines from the first two pentagons are carried forward to the third pentagon, except when two lines appear in the same position in the first two pentagons, in which case they are cancelled out

21. a) a cabbage

22. $-3 \times (12 \div 4) + 6 = -3 \times 3 + 6 = -3$

23. cabalistic

24. BLACKTHORN

25. HOUSE: SUMMERHOUSE/HOUSEHOLD

26. B: the diamond is shown pointing north, south, east and west

27. 19: it is the square root of the number formed by the digits 361. 16 is the square root of 256 and 17 the square root of 289.

28. a) offspring

29. FENNEL, CARROT

30. d) a dealer

31. pugnacious

32. BREECHES BUOY

33. disclaim, disavow

34. FRITTER

35. BEAUJOLAIS

36. concise, wordy

37. CHAIN: BICYCLE CHAIN/CHAIN GANG

38. d) a metal disk

39. A

40. 3: the numbers in the middle circle are the sum of the numbers in the same position in the other two circles

Test Seven: Questions

1.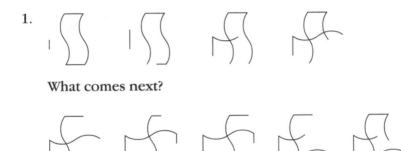

   What comes next?

A	B	C	D	E

2. What number should replace the question mark?

   2.5, 4.25, ? , 7.75, 9.5

3. Below are seven synonyms of the keyword NOTABLE. Take one letter in turn from each of these synonyms to spell out a further synonym of NOTABLE. All letters appear in the correct order.

   celebrated, famous, striking, renowned, rare, unusual, outstanding

4. Which number is the odd one out?

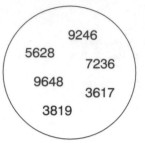

5. Overrun is to infest as overwhelm is to which of: imbricate, surmount, inundate, domineer, satiate?

6. Change one letter only from each word below to produce a familiar phrase.

    see tail

7. Alf is one and a quarter times as old as Jim, and Jim is one and a quarter times as old as Sid. The total of their ages is 61. How old are Sid, Jim and Alf?

8.

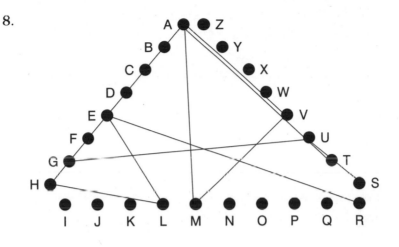

Find the starting point and track from letter to connected letter to spell out the name of a classical composer.

9.

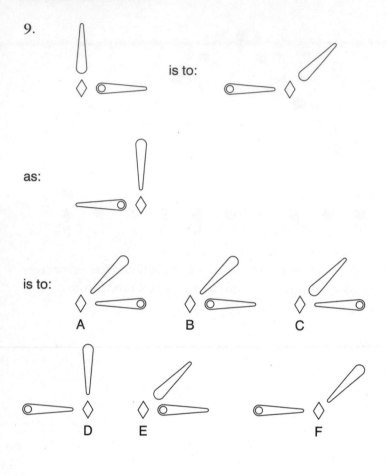

10.

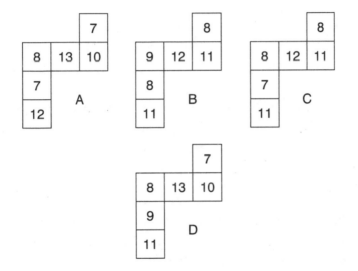

Which is the missing section?

11. Use every letter of the phrase GREAT PACIFIC HOP once each only to spell out the names of three fruit.

12. Which is the odd one out?

fathom, study, unravel, decipher, resolve

13. What number should replace the question mark?

    78   (243)   29

    16   (74)   14

    32   (?)   22

14.
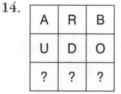

A	R	B
U	D	O
?	?	?

Start at one of the corner squares and spiral clockwise round the perimeter to spell out a nine-letter word finishing at the centre square. You must provide the missing letters.

15. The clues *shooting star/distant* (6,6) lead to a pair of words that are anagrams of each other: *meteor/remote*. To what pair of words (8,8) that are anagrams of each other do the clues *unnerving/borderline* lead?

16. Which is the odd one out?

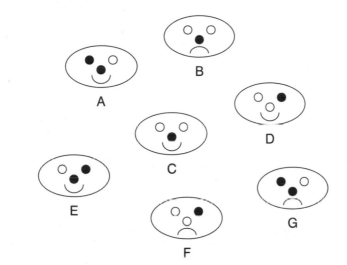

17.

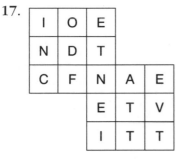

I	O	E		
N	D	T		
C	F	N	A	E
		E	T	V
		I	T	T

Arrange the letters in each square to spell out a nine-letter word. The two words are antonyms.

18. Insert two letters into each pair of brackets so that they finish the word on the left and start the word on the right. The letters in the brackets, reading in pairs downwards, will spell out an eight-letter word.

    LA (- -) EP

    HE (- -) ID

    RI (- -) IN

    DE (- -) GE

19. What number should replace the question mark?

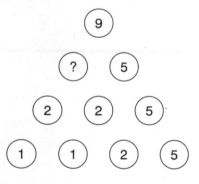

20.

    A   B   C   D   E   F   G   H

    What letter is two to the right of the letter four to the left of the letter three to the right of the letter C?

21. What is a *rill?*

    a) a young pig

    b) a fold in a cloth

    c) a small stream

    d) a design on a dress

22.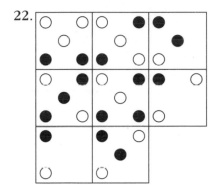

    Which is the missing box?

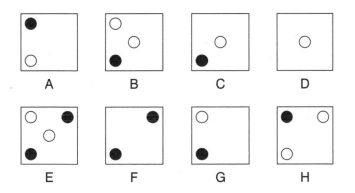

A B C D

E F G H

23. Which of these words is the opposite of *modesty*?

    disrespect, pretension, adequate, espouse

24. What is an *aconite*?

    a) ganoid

    b) a plant

    c) tongue

    d) braise

25. Fill in the missing letters to produce the name of a fruit:

    – – – TAR – – –

26. Simplify:

    $-7 \times 4 + 2 \times 3$

27. Which is the odd one out?

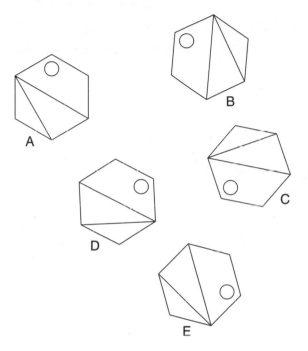

28. Which of these words means the same as *obviate*?

    custom, fulfil, frugal, preclude

29.   368421   is to   638241

    and   749135   is to   479315

    therefore   841263   is to   ?

30. Fill in the missing letters to produce the name of some-
    thing edible:

    – – – O – – AI – E

31. 3 8 5 9 2 7 6 8 9 2 5 7 6 3 2 5

Multiply by seven the number of times that an odd number is immediately followed by an even number in the list above. What is the answer?

32.

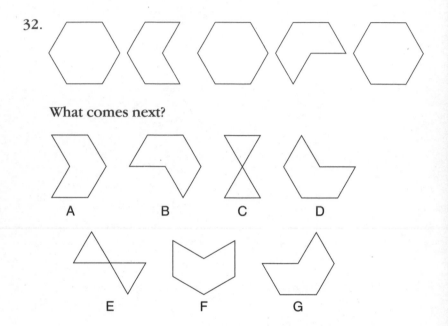

What comes next?

A	B	C	D

E	F	G

33. Which letter is two to the left of the letter immediately to the right of the letter four to the left of the letter G?

ABCDEFGH

34. What comes next?

100, 92.25, 84.5, 76.75, ?

35. Fill in the missing letters to produce a building term:

    – – – USTR – – –

36.

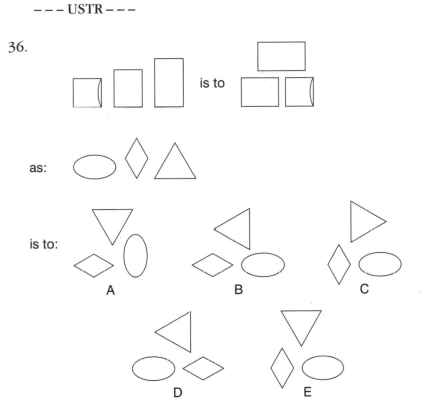

37. What is to *placate*?

    a) pacify

    b) hew rock

    c) build a wall

    d) set up a table

38. Three of the four pieces below can be fitted together to form a perfect square. Which is the odd piece out?

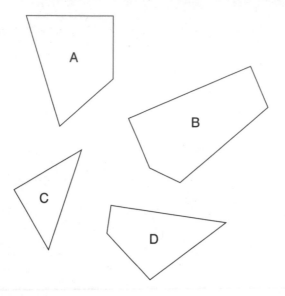

39. What is a *poundal*?

    a) unit of force

    b) dish of fruit

    c) rock face

    d) sea breeze

40. Solve the anagram in brackets to complete the quotation correctly. Writing about music is like dancing about (ERECT HAIRCUT).

Test Seven: Answers

1. C: the horizontal figure is disappearing by half a side at each stage and the vertical figure is appearing by half a side at each stage

2. 6: add 1.75 each time

3. eminent

4. 3617: in all the others the number formed by the last two digits is half the number formed by the first two digits

5. inundate

6. set sail

7. Sid 16, Jim 20, Alf 25

8. GUSTAV MAHLER

9. A: the top figure moves 45° clockwise and the figure with the circle slides over from left to right

10. B: looking across the numbers progress +3, −1. Looking down they progress −1, +3.

11. APRICOT, FIG, PEACH

12. study

13. 130: $(32 \times 2) + (22 \times 3)$

14. BODYGUARD

15. alarming/marginal

16. E: A is the same face as G but smile/frown, similarly B = C and F = D

17. CONFIDENT, TENTATIVE

18. STARCHED: LAST/STEP, HEAR/ARID, RICH/CHIN, DEED/EDGE

19. 4: from the top, $9 \times 5 = 45$, $45 \times 5 = 225$ and $225 \times 5 = 1125$

20. D

21. c) a small stream

22. G: only dots that appear in the same position twice in the first two squares are carried forward to the final square; however, they then change from black to white and vice versa

23. pretension

24. b) a plant

25. NECTARINE

26. $(-7 \times 4) + (2 \times 3) = -28 + 6 = -22$

27. A: the rest are the same figure rotated

28. preclude

29. 481623: the first and second numbers and the fourth and fifth numbers reverse

30. MAYONNAISE

31. 42

32. B: each alternate figure rotates 90° clockwise

33. B

34. 69: deduct 7.75 at each stage

35. BALUSTRADE

36. B: the figure on the bottom left moves to bottom right, the figure on the right rotates 90° and goes to the top and the figure in the middle rotates 90° and goes to bottom left

37. a) pacify

38.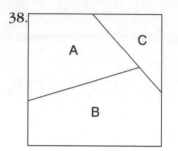

d) is the odd one out

39. a) unit of force

40. ARCHITECTURE

Test Eight: Questions

1.

What comes next?

   A   B   C   D   E

2. Which of these words is closest in meaning to *suppurate*?

   discharge, overthrow, materialize, outshine, astonish

3. My watch was correct at midnight after which it began to lose 14 minutes per hour until 7 hours ago it stopped completely. It now shows the time as 3.50 am. What now is the correct time?

4. Complete the six words so that the two letters that end the first word also start the second word, and the two letters that end the second word start the third word, and so on. The two letters that end the sixth word are the first two letters of the first word, thus completing the circle.

   $--$ LL $--$

   $--$ IS $--$

   $--$ ER $--$

   $--$ RA $--$

   $--$ NU $--$

   $--$ DU $--$

5. Which word is missing from the brackets that means the same as both definitions either side of the brackets?

   push to the limit (　　　) ancestry

6. In four years' time the combined age of me and my two daughters will be 107. What will it be in five years' time?

7. dopiness, uncloaking, dishwasher

   Which word below has something in common with the words above?

   gallant, crossfire, whirlwind, assault

8. Which is the odd one out?

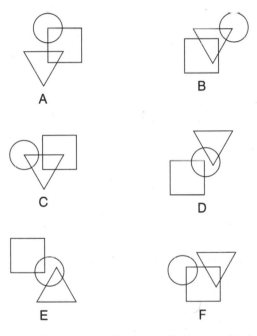

A

B

C

D

E

F

9. Petal is to corolla as stalk is to which of: stamen, nectary, anther, pedicel, pistil?

10. What number should replace the question mark?

   100, 87.6, 75.2, 62.8, 50.4, ?

11. Find two of the three words WAVE – CATTLE – GUISE that can be paired to form an anagram, which is a synonym of the remaining word. For example, with LEG – MEEK – NET, the words LEG and NET form an anagram of GENTLE, which is a synonym of the remaining word, MEEK.

12. What number should replace the question mark?

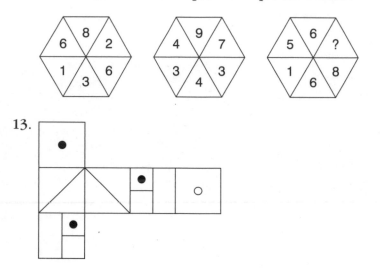

13.

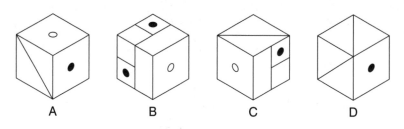

When this shape is folded to produce a cube, which is the only one of the following that *cannot* be produced?

A   B   C   D

14. Solve the cryptic clue. The answer is an 11-letter word anagram within the clue.

    Inside party reorganised for regular pay

15. Change one letter only in each word to produce two words that are opposite in meaning.

    die push

16. Fill in the missing numbers.

8		14		20	23	26		?
6	9	12		18		24		?
4		10	13	16		22	?	?
2		8		14		20		?

17. Only one group of six letters below can be rearranged to spell out a six-letter word in the English language. What is the word?

    GEMILO

    WAINTA

    BUDACO

    LITERA

    FOLAPI

18. Which is the odd word out?

    aggregate, ensemble, complement, compartment, integral

19.

T	1E 2S	1S 1W
1E 1S	1N 1W	2W 1S
1E 2N	2N 1E	1N 2W

```
        N
        |
W ------+------ E
        |
        S
```

Find the starting point and follow the instructions to finish at the square marked T. Every square must be visited just once.

1N

2W

means 1 square north then 2 squares west.

20. Which of the following is **not** an anagram of *roly poly pudding*?

    duly drip polygon

    pop drying loudly

    loudly dry piping

    or oddly lying pup

    pin glory up oddly

21. Fill in the missing letters to produce the name of a tree:

    – – – ALYP – – –

22. In how many ways can the word PATH be read? Start at the central letter P and move to an adjoining letter up, down, backward or forward, in and out in any direction.

```
                    H
            H       T       H
      H     T       A       T       H
H     T     A       P       A       T       H
      H     T       A       T       H
            H       T       H
                    H
```

23. What number should replace the question mark?

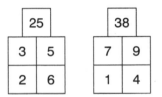

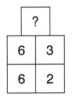

24. Ample is to substantial as grandiose is to which of: considerable, monumental, bulky, voluminous, large?

25. Which two of these words are most similar in meaning?

    mendicant, mediate, beggar, recluse, confederant, deity

26. Which two of these words are most similar in meaning?

    imbue, imagine, bathe, fragile, fragment, bluster

27.
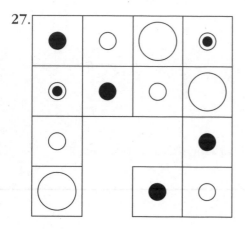

Which is the missing piece?

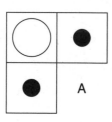

A

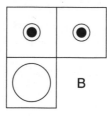

B

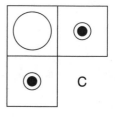

C

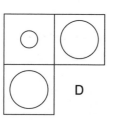

D

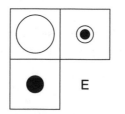

E

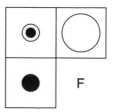

F

28. Find two words (5, 6) in this diagram. Letters are traced across the circle by chords. If the next letter is four letters or less away it will be found by tracing around the circumference. Clue: this is no place for a naturist in a theatre.

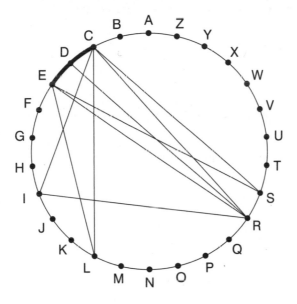

29. What number should replace the question mark?

1		4		?
5	3	7	2	4
7		1		2

30. Make a seven-letter word out of these four letters:

A T N C

31. Which of these words is nearest in meaning to *lethargy*?

    immunity, inactive, candour, tendency

32. Which of these words is not a nautical term?

    windlass, thimble, half-hitch, stigma

33. Find a word which when placed on the end of the first word and the start of the second makes two new words or phrases:

    CHIMNEY (– – –) ROAST

34. What number should replace the question mark?

4	1	7	2
1	6	0	3

9	5	6	8
7	5	4	?

35. Fill in the missing letters to produce the name of an article of clothing:

    – – B – Y – O – – S

36. Simplify:

    $$\frac{17}{18} \div \frac{34}{9} \div \frac{51}{3} =$$

37. beetle, moth, shark

    What word can precede the words above and follow the word below?

    paper

38. 3471   ????

    5005   7486

    1534   2589

    9221   4782

    7687   2193

    What number should replace the question marks?

39.

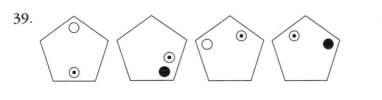

What comes next?

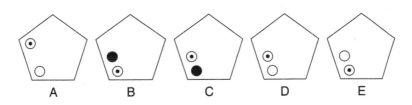

40. What number should replace the question mark?

    69, 138, 276, ? , 1104

Test Eight: Answers

1. E: the skip moves from leg to leg and the mouth alternates smile/sad/straight, and each arm goes up and down in turn

2. discharge

3. 12 noon:

    midnight   = midnight

    1 am   = 12.46

    2 am   = 1.32

    3 am   = 2.18

    4 am   = 3.04

    5 am   = 3.50

    plus 7 hours = 12 noon

4. CELLAR, ARISEN, ENERGY, GYRATE, TENURE, REDUCE

5. strain

6. 122: in another five years we will each be five years older i.e. $5 \times 3 = 15$, and $107 + 15 = 122$

7. crossfire: they all contain a tree: do**pine**ss, un**cloak**ing, dishw**ash**er – cross**fire**

8. E: in all the others the triangle is upside down

9. pedicel

10. 38: deduct 12.4 each time

11. GESTICULATE: WAVE

12. 3: $56 \times 3 = 168$. Similarly $68 \times 2 = 136$ and $49 \times 7 = 343$.

13. D

14. stipendiary (inside party)

15. din, hush

16.

8		14		20	23	26		32
6	9	12		18		24		30
4		10	13	16		22	25	28
2		8		14		20		26

Numbers in columns down reduce by 2, numbers in connected rows across increase by 3

17. LITERA = RETAIL

18. compartment: the others are the whole, a compartment is just a part of the whole

19.
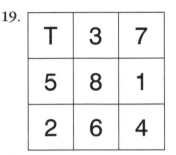

T	3	7
5	8	1
2	6	4

20. loudly dry piping

21. EUCALYPTUS

22. 28

23. 21: $(6 \times 2) + 3 + 6$. Similarly, $(3 \times 6) + 5 + 2 = 25$

24. monumental

25. mendicant, beggar

26. imbue, bathe

27. C: so that each vertical and horizontal line contains one each of the four different circle combinations

28. DRESS CIRCLE

29. 9: $157 \times 3 = 471$. $471 \times 2 = 942$

30. CANTATA

31. inactive

32. stigma

33. POT: CHIMNEYPOT/POT ROAST

34. 8: in each array the bottom row is the reverse of the top row minus 1

35. BOBBY SOCKS

36. $\dfrac{17}{18} \div \dfrac{34}{9} \div \dfrac{51}{3} = \dfrac{17}{18} \times \dfrac{9}{34} \times \dfrac{3}{51} = \dfrac{3}{204} = \dfrac{1}{68}$

37. tiger

38. 4897: in each array add the first and third numbers to obtain the second number, and the third and fifth numbers to obtain the fourth number

39. D: at each stage the dot with the circle moves one side anti-clockwise. The other dot moves two corners clockwise and alternates white/black.

40. 552: the numbers double at each stage

Test Nine: Questions

1. Identify two numbers between 1 and 60 which both meet all the following conditions:

   they are divisible by 3

   when the digits are added together the total is between 4 and 8

   they are odd numbers

   when the digits are multiplied together the total is between 4 and 8.

2.

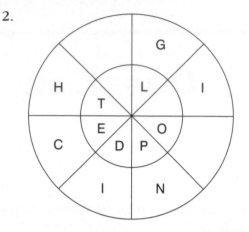

Find two eight-letters words which are antonyms, reading round the circles. One reads clockwise round the outer circle and one reads anticlockwise round the inner circle. You have to provide the missing letters.

3. Which is the odd one out?

    cylinder, cube, pentagon, tetrahedron, sphere

4. Find two of the three words SEE – RULER – ROVING that can be paired to form an anagram, which is a synonym of the remaining word. For example, with LEG – MEEK – NET the words LEG and NET form an anagram of GENTLE, which is a synonym of the remaining word, MEEK.

5.

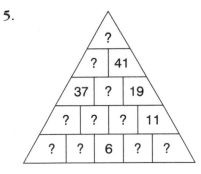

Each number in the pyramid is the sum of the two numbers immediately below it. Fill in the pyramid with the missing numbers.

6. What familiar phrase is indicated by the arrangement of letters below?

C

O   N

F   E   R

E   N   C   E

7. What number should replace the question mark?

4	4	2	2	5	2
2	1	4	3	1	3
?	6	0	4	3	4

8.

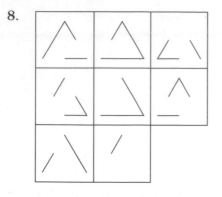

Which is the missing tile?

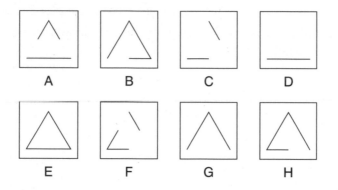

9. What number should replace the question mark?

1, 2, 4, 6, 9, 12, 15, 19, 23, 27, 31, ?

10. Avowed is to self-confessed as autodidact is to which of: self-motivated, self-taught, self-service, self-destructive, self-opinionated?

11. Place the letters in the correct segments in each quadrant to obtain two eight-letter words, both reading clockwise, which form a familiar phrase.

NW: RYTE

NE: LUAH

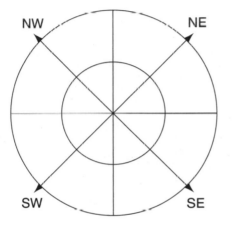

SE: ITIM

SW: VIED

12. Which letter is missing?

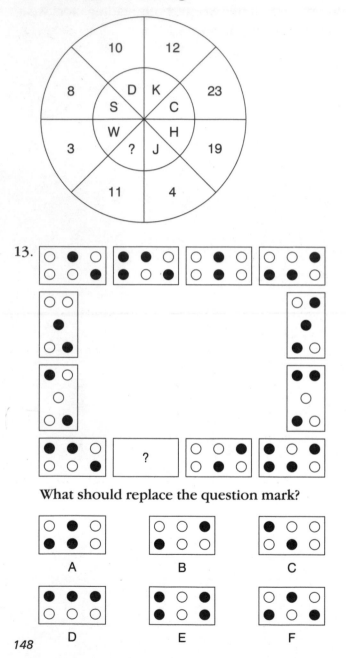

13.

What should replace the question mark?

A

B

C

D

E

F

14. Which two words below are closest in meaning?

    delectable, luxuriant, magnificent, plentiful, energetic, sanguine

15. What number should replace the question mark?

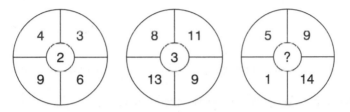

16. SEA POST OK is an anagram of which familiar phrase (3 words)? Clue: as one might put it.

17. Which word is missing from the brackets that means the same as both definitions either side of the brackets?

    mound (   ) column of timber or concrete used as a foundation

18. What comes next?

    96421, 13469, 96441, 15469, ?

19. Solve the cryptic clue. The answer is a 13-letter word anagram within the clue.

    Arrange his stingy loan bewilderingly

20.

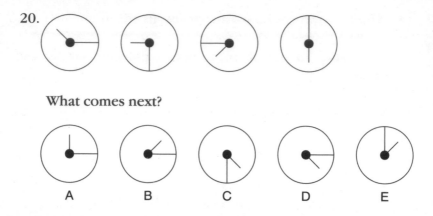

What comes next?

A	B	C	D	E

21. Which two of these words are synonyms?

   compliance, supernumary, maintain, wishful, agreement, pursue

22. Find one word (10) in this diagram. Letters are traced across the circle by chords. If the next letter is four letters or less away it will be found by tracing around the circumference. Clue: a royal bird?

23. Which two of these words are synonyms?

    altercation, desolate, entertain, restricted, repugnant, wrangle

24. Fill in the missing letters to produce the name of an appliance:

    – – – CRAC – – –

25. What is a *rondeau*?

    a) a plain

    b) a roundabout

    c) a poem

    d) a castle

26. Fill in the missing letters to produce building terms:

    a) – R – H – A –

    b) – I – R – R –

    c) – A – S – O –

    d) – H – M – E –

27. Make a seven-letter word out of these five letters:

    D Y A W R

28. Fill in the missing numbers. The link between the three numbers in each line is the same.

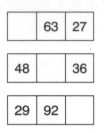

	63	27

48		36

29	92	

29. Four of the five pieces below can be fitted together to form a perfect circle. Which is the odd piece out?

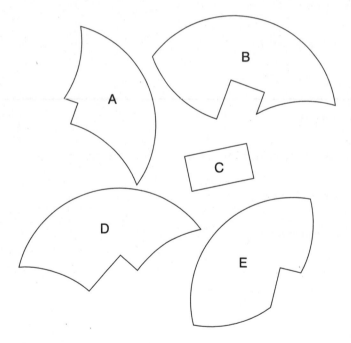

30. What number is missing?

784, 588, 440, ? , 60

31. Fill in the missing letters to produce a word meaning someone who copies manuscripts:

    – – – NUEN – – S

32. Find two words (7, 5) in this figure. Letters are traced across the circle by chords. If the next letter is four letters or less away it will be found by tracing around the circumference. Clue: a very colourful fish.

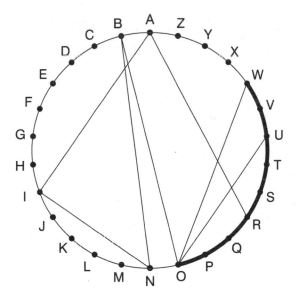

33. Find a word which, when placed on the end of the first word and the start of the second, makes two new words or phrases:

    FOUNTAIN (– – –) PAL

34. What is the meaning of *milch*?

    a) watery swill for cattle

    b) giving milk

    c) new straw

    d) horse fodder

35. Fill in the missing letters to produce the name of a kitchen appliance:

    – – – COLA – – –

36.

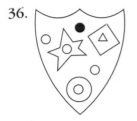

Which shield has most in common with the shield above?

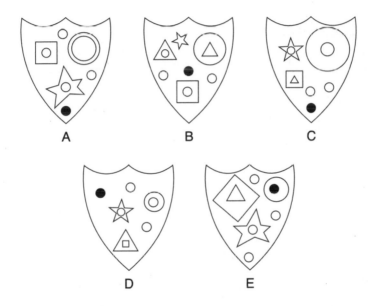

A   B   C

D   E

37. What is the longest word in the English language that can be produced from the 10 letters below? No letter can be used more than once.

BELMCAYOIT

38. What number should replace the question mark?

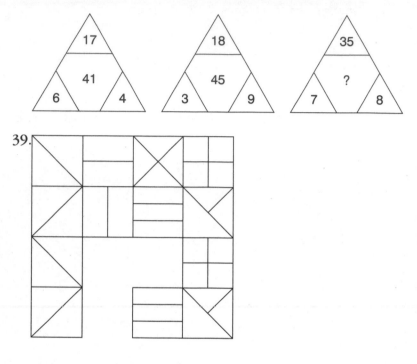

39.

Which is the missing piece?

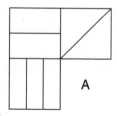

A

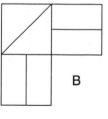

B

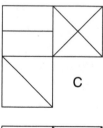

C

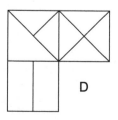

D

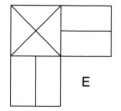

E

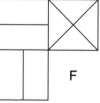

F

40. Fill in the missing letters to produce the name of a term that sometimes describes the weather:

    – – – NGEA – – –

Test Nine: Answers

1. 15 and 51

2. hygienic, polluted

3. pentagon: all the rest are solids

4. SOVEREIGN, RULER

5.

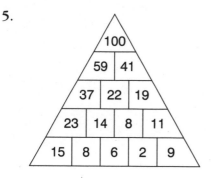

6. summit conference

7. 2: each group of four numbers around the dots totals 11

8. G: lines are carried forward from the first two squares in each row and column to the third square; however, where two lines appear in the same position in the first two squares they are cancelled out.

9. 36: +1, +2, +2, +3, +3, +3, +4, +4, +4, +4, +5

10. self-taught

11. RELATIVE HUMIDITY

12. L: look across at the number 12 directly opposite. The letter L is the twelfth letter of the alphabet. Similarly W is the 23rd letter etc.

13. E: diagonally opposite rectangles have identical dot arrangements but with black/white reversal

14. luxuriant, plentiful

15. 7: $5 \times 14 = 70$; $9 + 1 = 10$. $70 \div 10 = 7$

16. so to speak

17. pile

18. 96461: each number is the reverse of the previous number but with the same digit increased by 1 each time

19. astonishingly (his stingy loan)

20. D: the short hand moves 45° anticlockwise and the long hand moves 90° clockwise at each stage

21. compliance, agreement

22. KINGFISHER

23. altercation, wrangle

24. NUTCRACKER

25. c) a poem

26. a) ARCHWAY b) LIBRARY c) MANSION d) CHIMNEY

27. WAYWARD

28.

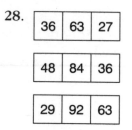

| 36 | 63 | 27 |

| 48 | 84 | 36 |

| 29 | 92 | 63 |

Reverse the first number then take the difference

29.

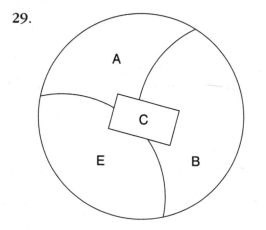

30. 160: $7 \times 84 = 588$, $5 \times 88 = 440$, $4 \times 40 = 160$, 1×60 $= 60$

31. AMANUENSIS

32. RAINBOW TROUT

33. PEN: FOUNTAIN PEN/PEN PAL

34. b) giving milk

35. PERCOLATOR

36. C: it has a circle in a star, a triangle in a square, a circle in a circle, and two more white dots and a black dot

37. metabolic

38. 91: $(7 \times 8) + 35$

39. F: so that the first and third lines are the same as the second and fourth lines

40. CHANGEABLE

Test Ten: Questions

1.

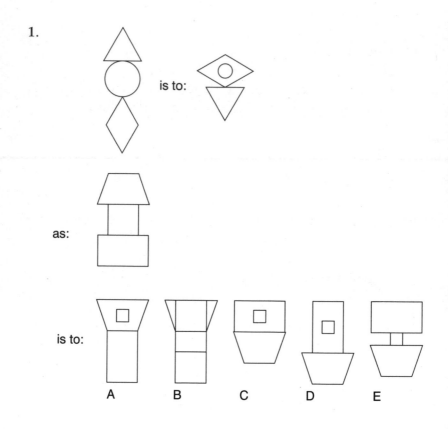

is to:

as:

is to:

A   B   C   D   E

2.

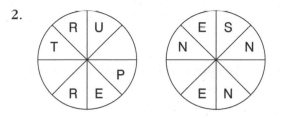

Find two words that are synonyms. One reads clockwise round one circle and the other reads anticlockwise round the other. You have to provide the missing letters.

3. A manufacturer produces widgets, but not to a very high standard. In a test batch of 18, 7 were defective. Then the manufacturer carried out a longer production run in which 567 of 1500 were defective. Had it improved its performance after the test run?

4. Which is the odd one out?

   trawler, felucca, sloop, dhow, dinghy

5. If the clue *spacious heath* (5,4) leads to the two-word palindrome *roomy moor* (that is, it reads the same both backwards and forwards), what two-word palindrome does the clue *burst forth flawless* (5,4) lead to?

6. Jill and Jack share the same birthday. Jill is three times as old as Jack is now, but in five years' time she will only be twice as old. How old was Jill when she was six times as old as Jack?

7. Change the position of four of the words in the sentence below so that it makes complete sense.

    It is necessary for us all to possess basic self-esteem skills in order to see us through the day, in order to protect our assertiveness and to provide a shield with which to maintain ourselves.

8. Which is the odd one out?

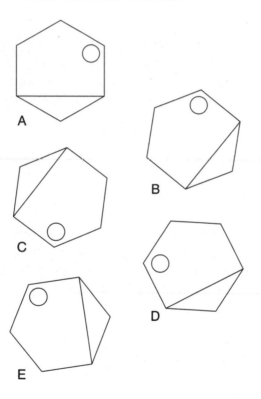

9. Aubergine is to eggplant as zucchini is to which of: cassava, artichoke, courgette, capsicum, yam?

10. Which of the following is not an anagram of a type of vegetable?

    A SUGAR SPA

    EEL CRY

    THRICE OAK

    HIS GOBBLE

11 Complete the grid by placing numbers in the empty squares so that the calculations are correct both across and down.

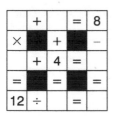

	+		=	8
×	■	+	■	−
	+	4	=	
=	■	=	■	=
12	÷		=	

12. Work from letter to adjacent letter horizontally and vertically (but not diagonally) to spell out a 12-letter word. You must provide the missing letters.

I	L	C	O
	O		S
A	N	O	

13.

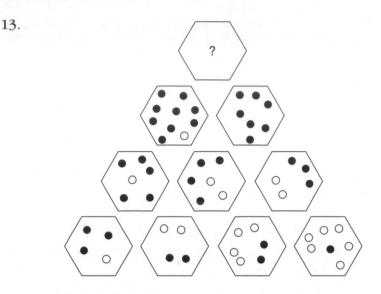

Which hexagon should appear at the top of the pyramid?

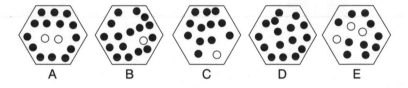

A   B   C   D   E

14. Which of these words is most opposite to *remiss*?

   sociable, faithful, extrinsic, scrupulous, sated

15. Which number should replace the question mark?

   1, 100, 8.5, ?, 16, 85, 23.5, 77.5

16. The following clue leads to which pair of rhyming words?

   common purpose

17. Which word, when placed in the brackets, will complete the word on the left and start the word on the right?

    CUI (   ) WY

18. Complete the bottom row of numbers.

4	6	12	9	3
16	21	7	18	15
23	25	31	28	39
54	59	62	56	53
?	?	?	?	?

19. A C F H K ? ?

    Which two letters continue the above sequence?

20.

1S 2E	1W 1S	1W 1S
1E 1S	1S 1E	T
2N 1E	1E 2N	2N 2W

Find the starting point and follow the instructions to finish at the square marked T. Every square must be visited just once.

1N

2W

means 1 square north then 2 squares west.

21. What is the meaning of *sudd*?

a) flying fox

b) floating vegetable matter

c) fair wind

d) sledge

22. Fill in the missing letters to produce the names of three vegetables:

    a) – P – O – T –

    b) – A – I – O –

    c) – A – B A G –

23. Find one word (10) in this diagram. Letters are traced across the circle by chords. If the next letter is four letters or less away it will be found by tracing around the circumference. Clue: pirates don't like these.

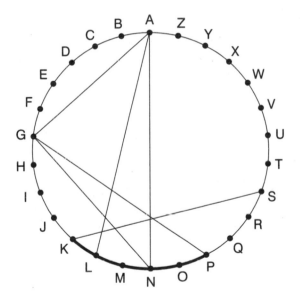

24. Fill in the missing letters to produce the name of a type of quartz:

    – H – L – E – O – Y

25. Find a word which, when placed on the end of the first word and the start of the second, makes two new words or phrases:

    FOOL (– – – – –) READER

26. Which is the odd one out?

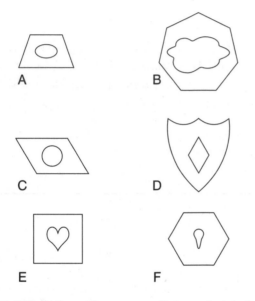

27. Work from letter to adjacent letter horizontally and vertically, but not diagonally, to spell out a 12-letter word. You must find the starting point and provide the missing letters.

Clue: negotiate the maze.

N	E	L	A
I	N	I	B
*	T	R	*

28. Which two pieces below can be fitted together to form a perfect square?

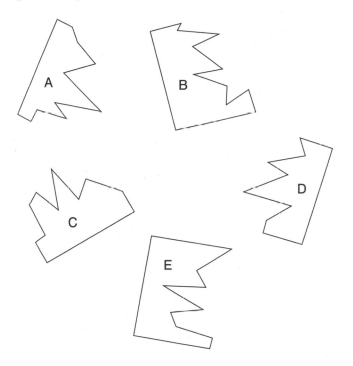

29. Find the two words that are most similar in meaning:

    sardonic, inceptive, ravenous, eternal, insatiable, fortuitous

30. Fill in the missing vowels to form a trite saying:

    TSBTT RTRTR TSNTH NTLT

31. Make one eight-letter word out of two of these blocks of four letters:

    PAVI TRUN PERS

    UADE LION CATE

32. Use every letter of the phrase REAR NEW BORN DOG once only to spell out three colours.

33. Find the two words that are antonyms:

    natural, riotous, manufactured, stubborn, create, occult

34. What is a *riband*?

    a) a fortress

    b) a bridge

    c) a ribbon

    d) a platoon

35. Find the two words that are most similar in meaning:

    recant, enumerate, advise, recollect, disown, epitomize

36. Jim won £30.00 on the horses, which meant he had five times more money than if he had lost £30.00. How much money had Jim before he won the £30.00?

37. Which is the odd one out?

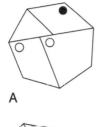

A

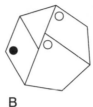

B

C

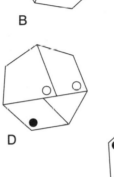

D

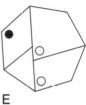

E

38. What is a *rumen*?

a) an animal's stomach

b) a whisper

c) the attic of a house

d) a starch

39. Fill in the missing letters to produce the name of a fish:

– – – TLEF – – –

40. Which of these words means the same as *fetter*?

fiduciary, shackle, infallible, discredit

Test Ten: Answers

1. D: the rectangle rotates 90° and goes to the top, the square goes inside the rectangle and the trapezium rotates 180° and goes to the bottom

2. trumpery, nonsense

3. Yes, but only very slightly:

    $7 \div 18 \quad = \quad 0.389$

    $567 \div 1500 = \quad 0.378$

4. trawler: the others are all sailing ships

5. erupt pure

6. 12: $12 - 2$

    $\quad 15 - 5$

    $\quad 20 - 10$

7. It is necessary for us all to possess basic **assertiveness** skills in order to see us through the day, in order to **maintain** our **self-esteem** and to provide a shield with which to **protect** ourselves.

8. D: the rest are the same figure rotated

9. courgette

10. HIS GOBBLE = BOBSLEIGH. The vegetables are ASPARAGUS, CELERY, ARTICHOKE.

11.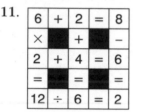

12. COSMOPOLITAN

13. B: the number of dots is determined by the number of dots in the two hexagon below. In the case of the black dots add the numbers together and in the case of the white dots take the difference.

14. scrupulous

15. 92.5: there are two interwoven sequences. In the first add 7.5 and in the other deduct 7.5.

16. same aim

17. SINE: CUISINE/SINEWY

18. 116 118 107 121 115. A + C = A (on the row below). Similarly: B + D = E, C + D = B, A + E = C, B + C = D.

19. M   P

    The sequence progresses: AbCdeFgHijKlMnoP

20.

8	2	5
3	6	T
1	4	7

21. b) floating vegetable matter

22. a) SPROUTS b) HARICOT c) CABBAGE

23. GANGPLANKS

24. CHALCEDONY

25. PROOF: FOOLPROOF/PROOFREADER

26. D: it is a straight-sided figure in a round-sided figure. The rest are round-sided figures inside straight-sided figures.

27. LABYRINTHINE

28.

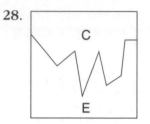

29. insatiable, ravenous

30. It is better to retire too soon than too late

31. PAVILION

32. BROWN, RED, ORANGE

33. natural, manufactured

34. c) a ribbon

35. recant, disown

36. £45.00: £45 + £30 = £75 and £45 − £30 = £15. (15 × 5 = 75)

37. B: the rest are the same figure rotated

38. a) an animal's stomach

39. CUTTLEFISH

40. shackle

Further Reading from Kogan Page

The Advanced Numeracy Test Workbook
ISBN 978 0 7494 3941 5

Aptitude, Personality & Motivation Tests
ISBN 978 0 7494 4179 1

The Aptitude Test Workbook
ISBN 978 0 7494 3788 6

A-Z of Careers & Jobs
ISBN 978 0 7494 4977 3

Career, Aptitude & Selection Tests
ISBN 978 0 7494 4819 6

Graduate Psychometric Test Workbook
ISBN 978 0 7494 4331 3

Great Answers to Tough Interview Questions
ISBN 978 0 7494 4356 6

How to Master Psychometric Tests
ISBN 978 0 7494 4279 8

How to Pass Advanced Aptitude Tests
ISBN 978 0 7494 3787 9

How to Pass Advanced Numeracy Tests
ISBN 978 0 7494 3791 6

How to Pass Advanced Verbal Reasoning Tests
ISBN 978 0 7494 4969 8

How to Pass the Civil Service Qualifying Tests
ISBN 978 0 7494 4853 0

How to Pass the GMAT
ISBN 978 0 7494 4459 4

How to Pass Graduate Psychometric Tests
ISBN 978 0 7494 4852 3

How to Pass the New Police Selection System
ISBN 978 0 7494 4946 9

How to Pass Numeracy Tests
ISBN 978 0 7494 4664 2

How to Pass Numerical Reasoning Tests
ISBN 978 0 7494 4796 0

How to Pass Professional Level Psychometric Tests
ISBN 978 0 7494 4207 1

How to Pass Selection Tests
ISBN 978 0 7494 4374 0

How to Pass Verbal Reasoning Tests
ISBN 978 0 7494 4666 6

How to Succeed at an Assessment Centre
ISBN 978 0 7494 4421 1

IQ and Aptitude Tests
ISBN 978 0 7494 4931 5

IQ and Personality Tests
ISBN 978 0 7494 4954 4

IQ and Psychometric Tests
ISBN 978 0 7494 5106 6

IQ and Psychometric Test Workbook
ISBN 978 0 7494 4378 8

The Numeracy Test Workbook
ISBN 978 0 7494 4045 9

Preparing the Perfect Job Application
ISBN 978 0 7494 5022 9

Preparing the Perfect CV
ISBN 978 0 7494 4855 4

Preparing the Perfect CV
ISBN 978 0 7494 4855 4

Readymade CVs
ISBN 978 0 7494 4274 3

Succeed at IQ Tests
ISBN 978 0 7494 5228 5

Successful Interview Skills
ISBN 978 0 7494 4508 9

Test Your IQ
ISBN 978 0 7494 4833 2

Test Your Numerical Aptitude
ISBN 978 0 7494 5064 9

Test Your Own Aptitude
ISBN 978 0 7494 3887 6

The Ultimate CV Book
ISBN 978 0 7494 3875 3

The Ultimate Interview Book
ISBN 978 0 7494 4310 8

The Ultimate IQ Test Book
ISBN 978 0 7494 4947 6

The Ultimate Job Search Book
ISBN 978 0 7494 4690 1

The Ultimate Psychometric Test Book
ISBN 978 0 7494 4458 7

Sign up to receive regular e-mail updates on Kogan Page books at
www.kogan-page.co.uk/signup.aspx and visit
our website: www.kogan-page.co.uk

ALSO AVAILABLE FROM KOGAN PAGE

ISBN: 978 0 7494 4969 8
Paperback 2008

ISBN: 978 0 7494 5229 2
Paperback 2008

ISBN: 978 0 7494 4421 1
Paperback 2005

ISBN: 978 0 7494 5064 9
Paperback 2007

ALSO AVAILABLE FROM KOGAN PAGE

ALSO AVAILABLE FROM KOGAN PAGE

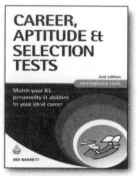

ISBN: 978 0 7494 4819 6
Paperback 2006

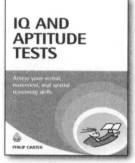

ISBN: 978 0 7494 4931 5
Paperback 2007

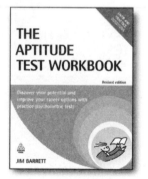

ISBN: 978 0 7494 5237 7
Paperback 2008

ISBN: 978 0 7494 3887 6
Paperback 2003

Sign up to receive regular email updates on
Kogan Page books www.kogan-page.co.uk/signup.aspx
and visit our website:

www.kogan-page.co.uk